she is...

Published in Atlanta, GA by She Is Ministries

Printed in the United States

Edited by Lindsay Williams
Cover Design and Interior Design by Sarah Siegand

ISBN: 9781093290066

she is...

COUNTERACTING THE ENEMY'S
LIES WITH GOD'S TRUTH

A 42-DAY *Devotional*

IVY CLEVELAND

Table of Contents

Introduction

Do you ever feel like you live in a world where everyone is telling you what you should do, be, and become? We compare our lives to perfect Pinterest boards and Instagram images that tell us we don't measure up. After all, our homes don't look like Joanna Gaines personally designed them. Our vacations will never be that exotic. And our kids, well I can never get mine to pose for a photo where everyone's looking at the camera at the same time. Or maybe that's just me.

We constantly tell ourselves we should strive to be better… perfect, even. But where does that leave us? It leaves us confused and broken, trying to understand why we don't fit the mold the world tells us we should fit into. Slowly, we begin to believe the lies comparison shouts at us: *You are not good enough. You are ugly. You will never amount to anything. No one loves you. Other wives do more than you.* The list goes on and on. But friend, I am here to tell you it's all a bunch of lies. Lies that will derail you from being the woman God has created you to be.

In order to be the women God has called us to be, we must call those lies out and counteract them with the truth God has set before us. Every. Single. Day. As you read this 42-day devotional, I want you to think of yourself in the third person. Wait, don't go anywhere. I'm not crazy, I promise. (At least, not in a I-hear-voices-psycho kind of way).

When you start to believe these lies, I want you to imagine God looking down on you and saying, "She is loved. She is beautiful. She is a warrior." And then you say it. Yes, to yourself. Out loud. That's right. For the next 42 days, I want the words He speaks over you to be the ones you repeat. I chose 42 days, because studies show it takes 21 days to break a habit and 21 days to start a new one. Ladies, we have got to break the habit of talking down to ourselves. Instead, let's adopt the habit of seeing ourselves as God sees us and believing His truth.

Yes girl, He loves you THAT much. He wants you to look in the mirror and see the beautiful woman He created. Rest assured, you are not alone in this crazy thing called life. Let's go through these next 42 days together and turn those lies into truths.

xoxo,

Ivy

She is Beautiful

"For you created me in my inmost being, you knit me together in my mother's womb. I praise you because I am fearfully and wonderfully made. Your works are wonderful. I know that full well."

PSALM 139:13-14

When I was a little girl, I was 100 percent sure I was a beautiful princess, and I believed I would one day marry my *handsome* prince. Looking back, I am 100 percent sure I married my (oh my word!) *handsome* prince, but I'm not so sure about the beautiful princess part anymore.

At what point did my view of myself change? Perhaps it was the day a boy called me "freckle face" at a water park. Maybe it was the day I realized I was pretty chubby, while other girls seemed so thin. Or maybe it was the day I found out boys existed, and soon realized they paid attention to all the other girls...but not me. Could it have been when I looked in the mirror after having baby number two and realized things were sagging where they once seemed a little more, shall we say, firm?

The devil loves it when we feel like we aren't beautiful. In fact, I think he plants tiny little seeds into our minds, giving us a million reasons why we are not beautiful. It doesn't help that there are now apps that will shrink, brighten, erase, and sculpt any flaw you see on your body. Those apps are of the devil, too. And now it's not enough for us to simply look at this fake, altered image of ourselves and have a good laugh. No, we then have to post it for the rest of the female population to aspire to.

Gals, we must recognize when the devil is feeding us lies. If we don't, they will begin to take root and grow. This is easier said than done, trust me. Knowing you're beautiful is basically a super power.

Think about it, the God of the universe formed you. He knit you together so perfectly, without any flaw or blemish. He doesn't look down on you and think, "That one right there? She's ugly." God, the Father, looks down on every one of His daughters and says, "Wow! What a beautiful masterpiece I have in her."

It's funny, once I started having kids of my own, I think I started looking at myself a little differently. Maybe it's because I began to see my children the way God sees His children. I would always say I hated my freckles (I blame the "freckle face" comment.), until I had a sweet little ginger baby who started getting freckles when he was about three. Honey, let me tell you, that boy will never hear his mama say she doesn't like freckles, because I would never want him to think they are anything less than angel kisses. (You know, the ones that sneak into his room at night and kiss him.) If you stop and think about it, isn't that what God is saying to us? Every freckle, every single strand of hair, every mole, every weird and wonderful characteristic that makes you YOU, He created and calls it beautiful.

Miranda Karr says, "A rose can never be a sunflower, and a sunflower can never be a rose. All flowers are beautiful in their own way. And that's like women, too."

Like flowers, God carefully created us in unique and different ways; and you know what, friend? That's OK. Know you are beautiful, because HE says you are.

Jesus, thank You for creating me. Thank You for looking down on me and loving what You see. Help me to see myself the way You see me. Help me to hold onto this truth today when the enemy attacks my self-worth. I am beautiful, because You say I am. Amen.

SAY IT: *I am Beautiful.*

READ IT: Psalm 139:13-14

WRITE IT: List 10 things you love about yourself. Come on, you got this!

She is Strong

"God is within her, she will not fall;
God will help her at break of day."

PSALM 46:5

Good ole Webster gives us two definitions for the word *strong*:

1) *having power to move heavy weights or perform other physically demanding tasks*
2) *able to withstand great force or pressure*

Without saying anything else, I would say those definitions pretty much sum up what being a woman is all about, wouldn't you? Yes girl, I hear you shouting at your book right now! Amen? I think, deep down, we know how strong we are. We know that when push comes to shove, we can rise up and stand our ground. But life gets frantic, and we tend to forget that.

The devil loves nothing more than to distract us with the

many demands of life. If he keeps us busy, we won't feel like we have time to get into God's Word. Sister, let me tell you the truth. Without His Word, your strength will run out; and you will be operating on fumes. Maybe that's you right now. Perhaps you're reading this saying, "Yep, that's definitely me. My giver has given out, and I am running on the little bit of fumes I can muster to make it to bed time." I would encourage you to pick that Bible up, grab a highlighter, and allow God to speak to you. Right now. His Word tells us when we are weak, He is strong.

Being a wife is hard. And we've all heard the oh-so-ever-true statement, "There ain't no hood like motherhood." Life gets brutal, ladies. But now's not the time to back down. When life is knocking you in every direction, turn your eyes to Jesus, and allow Him to renew your strength. We were created to withstand hard things. God created us to be fierce women of God. We can stand firm on His Word and allow His strength to rise up within us.

Don't you dare feel sorry for yourself today. You look at your day and tell it who's boss! Take control, and be that strong woman God created you to be. The sky's the limit, and there is nothing you can't do. Philippians 4:13 confirms that: "*I can do all things through Christ who gives me strength.*" You go girl, yes *you*!

Prayer

Sweet Jesus, thank You for creating me to withstand this ever-so-demanding life. Thank You that You have made me strong. Lord, today when I feel weak, let me cling to Your Word and know that I am who You say I am—strong in Jesus' name. Amen.

SAY IT: *I am Strong.*

READ IT: Psalm 46:1-5, Philippians 4:13,

WRITE IT: List three strengths you have. (Yes, the ability to make a good cup of coffee is for sure a strength! I'm putting that on my list!)

day 3

She is Enough

"For we are God's handiwork, created in Christ Jesus to do good works which God prepared in advance for us to do."
EPHESIANS 2:10

I don't know how grade school was for you, but for me, it was pretty brutal. I learned really quickly I was a loud and funny person. (Not much has changed in that area.) I would hide behind my wittiness to distract people from seeing how things truly hurt me. And while we're on the topic, why do we let said people tell us how skinny, pretty, or smart we should be? I mean, who died and made them king (or queen) anyway?

I will never forget the day a little punk (Is that allowed in a Christian book?) called my house, solely to leave a message on my answering machine (Yes, I realize I probably just dated myself.) He left a whiny little song on the machine: "Poison Ivy! Poison Ivy!" All the mamas out there can totally understand why my mama got dismissed from school the next day. Apparently, the school system gets concerned when a grown woman starts sizing up a fourth grade boy and asking to speak to him in the hallway.

I believe, as women, we all go through times in our lives when we just don't feel like we are enough. We compare ourselves to the mom whose gifting is organizing what she has organized. We hang our heads in shame as we carry in store-bought cookies to *another* classroom party, because we didn't have time to bake anything the night before. We look in the mirror and replay all the hurtful things people have said to us in the past. However, it's extremely important to understand God created us all very differently...on purpose. We all have a significant role to play. And girl, let me tell you this, you are enough for that role.

Stop allowing the enemy of your soul to lie to you. He wants you to doubt yourself. Stop looking at all the things you *can't* do, and start focusing on all the things you can do. Honestly, I am terrible at managing stress. It doesn't take long before I start wigging out, and my whole family thinks my body has been invaded by an unknown creature. But I have found I am really good at encouraging people. With every weakness you feel you have, God has placed a strength inside of you. Now, look at yourself in the mirror and say, "Girl, please, do you know who you are?" Feel better?

I could spend an entire book encouraging you that you are enough, but until you realize you are enough, you will continue to feel as though you will never measure up. Hear this truth: You are beautiful enough, strong enough, smart enough, and brave enough. That is truth! Believe it, girl!

Prayer

Lord, thank You for who You are. Thank You for living inside of me and making me enough. Thank You for choosing me. You, the God who created the universe, chose me. Help me to see today that I am enough, and that all I need is found in You.
In Jesus' name, amen.

SAY IT: *I am Enough.*

READ IT: Ephesians 2:10, Romans 8:1-4

WRITE IT: What are some scenarios where you don't feel enough? Write them down. Then beside each one, write, "… but I am enough."

day 4

She is Purposeful

"There is a time for everything, and a season for every activity under the heavens."

ECCLESIASTES 3:1

*G*irl, did you know God has a specific plan for you? There will be days when you doubt that. There will be days when you'll ask yourself why you exist. On those days, please remember these words: You have a purpose. If the Bible tells us there is a time for everything, we have to give ourselves permission to have seasons of all kinds.

You will have seasons of mourning, happiness, planting, receiving, embracing, and refraining. It's important that we recognize what season we are in, so that we can give it purpose. My pastor says this: "Everyone is either about to walk *into* a storm, in the middle of a storm, or coming out of a storm." It's true! Remember the story in the Gospels about the time Jesus calmed the storm? Before He calmed it, Jesus led the disciples into the storm. He knew what was about to happen, yet He kept on sleeping in the back of the boat. How much freedom could we embrace if we understood that nothing happens to us without Jesus already knowing?

If you find yourself in a hard season right now, don't despise it; embrace it. Allow God to teach you the purpose of this season. Let's be women who wake up each morning with tenacity, believing that today could be the day Jesus stands up in our boat and calms the storm. We serve a purposeful God, who not only loves His children as a whole, but as individuals.

In order to walk in purpose each and every day, we must believe God wants what's best for us—yesterday, today, and tomorrow. Our Father works all things together for our good and His glory.

I saw a quote recently that I fell in love with that speaks about purpose: "Your life has a purpose. Your story is important. Your dreams count. Your voice matters. You were born to make an impact."

Sister, you matter. You are important. You have a purpose. Don't sit on the sidelines of life any longer. Get in the game, and do something to change the world!

Prayer

Father, I pray You would settle my mind today. Help me to see the purpose in my pain. God, help me in this difficult season to remember You are in my boat, and at any moment, my storm could stop raging. You are so faithful to me, and I trust You in all things. Thank You for creating me with a special purpose. Amen.

SAY IT: *I am Purposeful.*

READ IT: Ecclesiastes 3:1-8

WRITE IT: Make a list of some dreams God has given you. Pray over your dream list tonight, and see what God will do with them!

day 5

She is Pure

"Blessed are the pure in heart, for they will see God."
MATTHEW 5:8

*W*hen you hear the word purity, what's the first thing that comes to mind? For me, it's the purity conference I went to as a teenager. The whole event was centered around a lady telling us it was God's plan to not have sex until we were married. I wish I could tell you her lesson stuck, and I was completely abstinent until I got married.

I want to make myself very clear on this issue. Bottom line, the Bible tells us we are to wait until we are married to have sex. God makes that clear. It doesn't matter if you are a certain age or if you've been married before. God still expects you to abstain from sex until marriage. I realize this viewpoint is not popular in our culture today, but ladies, we can't water down our faith, and this is part of it—even if it's an unpopular stance.

Sex is certainly a big part of purity, but I believe there are other ways God wants us to be pure, too. What about purity in the way we dress? What about purity in what we read? What about purity in what we watch? You and I live in a world that bombards us with inappropriate entertainment. The devil knows if he can get into our minds, he's halfway to a victory. We have to be women who guard not only our hearts, but our eyes and ears, too.

A few years ago, a book came out that was marketed as a "romance novel." It quickly became the book that every woman in America was reading. The media called it a "love story." It was a love story, indeed, but it was also a porno under the guise of a bestseller. As I gave into the pressure of, "Well, other wives are reading it!" I quickly realized I was reading something that went against everything I stood for. I allowed the pages of the book to fill my mind with images I knew were inappropriate. It made me uncomfortable, and I knew the Holy Spirit was convicting me. In that moment, I had a choice to make. I could finish the book so I would have something to contribute when the popular novel came up in conversation, or I could be obedient, put the book down, and stop right there on that exact page. I'll admit, I get things wrong a lot, but I'm happy to say, in this particular instance, I got it right. I put the book down.

The devil is convincing. He'll tell us, "Just have a little fun! Don't be so serious all the time. What will it hurt for you to go watch a movie of men dancing and stripping with your girlfriends? I mean, it's just a night out, right?" WRONG! It starts with an "innocent" movie or "the book that everyone's reading," and then next thing you know, you're replaying those images in your head and wondering why your husband doesn't have abs of steel.

To be a pure woman is to have a pure heart. To have a pure heart, we must protect it from the enemy's schemes at all costs.

I know today's topic might not make me popular, but being a woman of purity is so crucial in your walk with the Lord. I knew I couldn't address the topic of biblical womanhood without discussing it. Let's make a pact to keep our eyes and ears on things that honor God and add beauty to our lives. I promise, purity is a path you won't regret.

God, I pray for the Holy Spirit's conviction. I pray You would remind me of the times I have been impure. I want to be a woman who is pure and pleasing in Your sight. Show me the areas of my life where I need to make some changes. In Your name I pray, amen.

SAY IT: *I am Pure.*

READ IT: Matthew 5:8, 1 Peter 1:14-16, James 4:7-8

WRITE IT: Write down any areas in your life where you feel impure. Ask the Lord to help you submit these specific areas to Him.

day 6

She is Patient

"Be joyful in hope, patient in affliction, faithful in prayer."
ROMANS 12:12

The old saying remains true: "Never ask the Lord for patience unless you are ready to be tested." I'm pretty sure I failed a test in the grocery store the other day. Just picture it. I had my five-year-old, who asked a gazillion questions; and my two-year-old, who pretty much melts down anytime we leave the house. We finally made it to the register, and the lady in front of us gave me the evil eye because my bag of chips crossed the divider that separated my things from hers. Let's just say I had to rededicate my life to Jesus once we got in the car. (I'm kidding...kinda.)

To be willing to learn patience is to truly grow in the Lord. Patience is a sign of a mature believer. Even though the very thought of this topic makes me throw up a little in my mouth, patience is something we must ask the Lord for.

Patience takes a lot of forms. Patience is putting others first. Patience is keeping your cool when your child says "Mom!" for the millionth time in the last hour. Patience is smiling when the cashier is taking forever (and I do mean *forever*) to bag your groceries. Perhaps patience is waiting on Jesus to stand up in your boat and calm the raging storm. There are so many scenarios where patience is required in our lives. But, good grief, is it ever hard!

So how do we get to a place where learning patience is not such a grueling process? Spoiler alert! We don't! Learning patience is a life-long process. It's challenging, and it takes work. However, I believe patience is God's way of molding us into the women He desires for us to become. I believe patience is a crucial step in our becoming.

Don't be the woman who despises the learning process. Instead, be the woman who says, "I know God will give me the strength to endure whatever comes my way." Let's do this! I want to be THAT girl, don't you?

Prayer

Lord, I pray You would help me to have patience today. Jesus, I want to become the woman You have called me to be, so I do pray that with a sincere heart. Help me in this area. Be my strength when I am weak. Help me to show everyone that I come in contact with today that it's You who lives inside of me. Amen.

SAY IT: *I am Patient.*

READ IT: Proverbs 15:18, Romans 12:12, Psalm 40:1

WRITE IT: In what areas could you use a little more patience? (When I made this list, it was pretty long, but let's just start with five things and go from there. Baby steps, right?)

day 7

She is Passionate

"Whatever you do, work at it with all of your heart, as working for the Lord. Not for human masters."

COLOSSIANS 3:23

I love check lists, don't you? Doesn't it feel so good to put that check mark beside a completed task? Never mind that once I complete a task, I normally write something else down just so I can check it off, too. Unfortunately, I'm guilty of living my Christian life this way, as well.

- ✔ Read Bible today
- ✔ Prayed at least once (not just at meal time)
- ✔ Didn't lose my cool with my kids (well, that one's debatable)
- ✔ Met my husband's needs

God doesn't want our relationship with Him to be

dependent on a check list. God wants us to be passionate about serving Him in every area of our lives. He wants us to eagerly read His Word, pray, and live for Him; not because it's the "Christian" thing to do, but because our passion for Jesus is so strong, that all we do, we do for Him.

I have found in my own life that I'm the happiest when I live a passionate life serving Jesus. I remember passing by the TV in our living room one day and hearing Joyce Meyer saying, "Did you know you could sweep your floors with joy, as if you are serving God in the biggest way?" I'll be honest, my first response was an eye roll. There ain't nothing joyful about sweeping floors. (She must not have meant the floors that toddlers spend all day on.) But as I let this truth soak into my spirit, I realized she was right. Understanding this concept helped me find joy in the simplest things.

If we do everything as if we're doing it for Jesus, it cultivates passion. Even if that means doing a sixth load of laundry for the day. Whatever you find yourself stressing over today, ask yourself, "Am I doing this for man, or for God? Am I doing this just to get a check mark?"

No matter what season of life we are in, we can choose to make it the best one ever by passionately pursuing the tasks set before us for the glory of our Savior. You got this, friend!

Prayer

*Jesus, thank You for who You are. Thank You for giving
me a passion to serve You. Today, help me to find You in all
that I do—whether that be at home with my family, cleaning
house, or in my career. Help me to do all things as if I am
doing them for the King of Kings. I love You, Jesus.
Thank You for being so good to me. Amen.*

SAY IT: *I am Passionate.*

READ IT: Colossians 3:23, 1 Corinthians 10:31,

WRITE IT: What are you passionate about? Write down
your passions, and ask God to give you opportunities to do the
things you're passionate about.

day 8

She is Saved

"Salvation is to be found through him alone; in all the world there is no one else whom God has given who can save us."

ACTS 4:12

*H*ow amazing is it that God loved us so much that He would send His one and only Son to a world where He would be beaten, mocked, and crucified on a cross? He did all of this so we would have the opportunity to accept His Son and receive eternal life. The God of the universe unfolded His redemption plan simply because He longs for a direct relationship with His children (that's you and me!). WOW!

For me, the day I received that love was many, many years ago when I was only five years old. I will never forget that moment. I was playing with some dolls in my room, and I just felt a deep yearning to ask Jesus to come into my heart. I knew that the Jesus I was learning about in Sunday School was real and that I needed Him to save my soul.

I found my mom and asked her to pray with me. Right then and there, in our double-wide trailer, this girl received the greatest gift ever. A few weeks later, I got baptized in our small country church wearing a solid white dress, lacy white socks, and frilly gloves. I'm sure I was thrilled about this outfit.

I've since learned salvation is something no one can take away from you. Salvation guarantees eternal life with Jesus. It's the thing that assures you that, no matter what, Jesus Christ will always be your constant. Doesn't that news just make you want to hop out of your seat right now and take a few laps around your kitchen shouting? (Maybe that's just my charismatic roots showing.)

If you're reading this book, and you want to be the woman God created you to be, don't miss this crucial step. If you can't pinpoint a time when Jesus changed your life, then I would encourage you right now, wherever you are, to turn you heart to Jesus and receive His salvation. After you've prayed and asked Jesus to save you, tell someone! This kind of thing is not something to be silent about.

Actually, salvation is the very first step to becoming a strong, powerful, and God-fearing woman. Have you taken that foundational step?

Prayer

Jesus, thank You so much for loving me enough to come to a cruel world and to be crucified so that I might live with You forever. Salvation is a precious gift that no one can ever take from me. I am forever Yours! In Jesus' name, amen.

SAY IT: *I am saved.*

READ IT: Acts 4:12

WRITE IT: What is your salvation story? Write it down, and then share it with someone.

If you've never asked Jesus to be the Lord of your life, consider this:

"If you declare with your mouth that Jesus is Lord and believe in your heart that God raised him from the dead, you will be saved." Romans 10:9

1) Admit you are a sinner.
2) Believe Jesus is who He says He is. Jesus is the only way to the Father in heaven, and no one can be saved except through Him.
3) Confess you are a sinner in need of a Savior. Ask for His forgiveness. Repent and turn from your sin.

day 9

She is Submissive

"A woman should learn in quietness and full submission."
1 Timothy 2:11

The independent woman in me sees the word *submit* in the Bible and says, "I gotta do what now?" It's important that we realize our first obligation—and highest calling—is to submit to Jesus. We must submit our lives to Him and follow wherever He leads. When we allow God to teach us how to submit to His calling on our lives, then submitting to our husbands will not be so hard.

I know some of you are reading this chapter and thinking, "Girl, you don't know my husband. He is not worthy of my submission." You're right, I don't know your husband, but I know what God says in His Word. Here's the unmistakable truth: God calls wives to submit to their husbands, and he calls husbands to lay down their lives for their wives.

God created Adam *first*, then Eve. Whether we like it or

not, men are created to lead us. A man who is submitted to Christ will lead His family toward Christ, not away from Him. Unless your husband is wanting you to do something immoral, illegal, or unethical, it is your job to let him lead. I promise you, this will speak volumes to him; and your marriage will thrive as you let him fulfill his rightful role. This isn't to say that wives should be doormats. No sir! We're entitled to speak our minds, too! It's important that we don't let our own voices get diminished in a marriage. If your husband is following Christ, he'll also respect your opinion.

If your husband is not a Christ follower, pray for him, encourage him, love him, and most importantly, live for Jesus in front of him. Show him you support him by allowing him to lead. If you're single, don't think this is a topic you should just gloss right over. Being submissive to Christ and His leading now will actually help you when God does bring that man into your life who will one day become your husband. (Wait on him, girl! Don't you dare settle!)

Prayer

Father, teach me how to submit to Your leading. God, show me the areas in my life where I have not done so. Thank You for being my leader and for also equipping my husband to be the leader of our home. Help me, today, to submit to that leading with love and respect. In Jesus' name, amen.

SAY IT: *I am Submissive.*

READ IT: 1 Timothy 2:11, 1 Peter 3:1-6, Psalm 40:8

WRITE IT: Write out your prayers for your husband today. Submit those prayers to the Lord, and watch God transform your marriage. If you're single, make a list of traits you desire in a husband. Pray over those character traits, and give it to the Lord. Watch Him work. And again…wait on THE man, girlfriend!

day 10

She is Gentle

"Rather it should be the inner self, the unfaded beauty of a gentle and quiet spirit, which is of great worth in God's sight."

1 PETER 3:4

*M*y husband is a six-foot-two hunk of a man. When we first started dating, he often offended me by his roughness. When he grabbed things, it was rough. When he said things, it was rough. When he even ate, it was rough. That's when I promptly told him that I would be putting him through "Softening School." Softening School would be where he would learn how to approach things as a "gentle giant." I wish I could tell you he graduated a long time ago, but here we are 16 years later, and he's still learning. I will say he is much improved.

If I'm honest, I think we're all guilty of being rough with other people's feelings. If we're not careful, we'll hear ourselves utter phrases like, "Well, I'm just being honest..." or "No offense, but..." Then there's my personal favorite: the "laughing insult," where we use comedy to mask a real jab at another person. Yes, we are all humans with opinions; but the truth is, not everyone needs to hear them all the time. Not every thought that passes through your brain needs to be said out loud. As women of God, we need to learn how to cultivate a gentle spirit.

Jesus is so gentle with His daughters. He's patient and kind in His pursuit of us. He is quick to listen and slow to anger. These are the character traits we should model.

Rest assured, becoming a gentle woman will take work. It means holding your tongue when people deserve to be told they are wrong. It means staying silent when you want to talk. It means keeping insults to yourself. It means thinking before you speak. And some days, it will take everything in you to remain quiet or refrain from saying the very thing you want to scream. However, it can be done.

Let's be women other women actually want to be around. Women who build up instead of tearing down. Women who are gentle in the way we love, speak, correct, and teach. Let's practice extending the same love, grace and gentleness our heavenly Father extends to us.

Prayer

*Jesus, thank You for who You are. Thank You that You give me
the perfect example of what true gentleness looks like. You are so
kind to me. Today, help me to be kind to other people and show
them Your love. Help me to die to my selfish ways
and receive Your goodness. Amen.*

SAY IT: *I am Gentle.*

READ IT: Philippians 4:5, Psalm 103:8-11, 1 Peter 3:4

WRITE IT: Write down the names of two people who are
hard to be gentle with. Pray specifically for those people today.

day 11

She is Humble

*"Therefore as God's chosen people, holy and
dearly loved, clothe yourself with compassion, kindness,
humility, gentleness, and patience."*

COLOSSIANS 3:12

To be a humble woman is to recognize that nothing you do is a result of your own ability. A humble woman realizes it's God's power at work within her that allows her to accomplish anything in life—big or small.

It's easy to look at our talents and abilities and believe we are the ones who make things happen. Sister, let me tell you, God is at work in you whether you like it or not. You are not in control. Every gift, every talent, every accomplishment, every accolade and every good thing comes from the Lord above. We accomplish everything in His strength, not our own. When we allow seeds of arrogance to be planted in our spirits, pride takes root; and eventually, pride comes before the fall. And let me tell you, the fall will come.

God, however, wants better for His daughters. He wants us to remain humble. When we walk in humility, it changes our perspective. Humility allows us to stop comparing and start celebrating others. Humility helps us see that there's more than enough to go around. Humility also gives us eyes to see that each and every step in our lives is ordered by the One who created us.

I don't know about you, but I always tend to remember the moments in my life when I thought a little too much of myself. Those moments stand out very clearly in my memory. Looking back, every single time, my eyes were not fixed on Jesus, but on my own ability. It seems I was trying to do something in my own strength so that I could get all the credit and glory.

Now, don't hear me say that you should become a "Debbie Downer" and have no confidence. Quite the contrary, actually. There's a difference between arrogance and confidence. God wants us to be confident in His ability and who He created us to be. I think He just wants us to view ourselves as willing vessels, open to be used by Him in any way He leads. Apart from Him, we can do nothing; but with Him, all things are possible.

Prayer

God, keep me humble. I pray I would look around and see You in everything I say and do. Help me become a willing vessel to be used by You for Your glory. It is only by Your hand that I have the ability to do anything. In Your name I pray, amen.

SAY IT: *I am Humble.*

READ IT: James 4:10, Colossians 3:12

WRITE IT: Write out a Scripture verse or inspirational quote that reminds you to stay humble. Hang it somewhere you look every day (like your bathroom mirror) as a reminder to keep Jesus first.

day 12

She is Diligent

"Diligence is man's precious possession."
PROVERBS 12:27

*M*y husband is the most diligent person I have ever met. Diligence is a wonderful trait to possess, except when we are having what I like to call "intense fellowship." I'm like, "OK, it's over. I don't need to understand why you made the decision you made. Just know you upset me, say you're sorry, and let's move on." But no, not my precious, diligent husband. He is going to explain in full detail how we got to this place of disagreement. We will discuss how we can fully solve the problem, and then and only then, will we stop talking.

Bless his heart, he is so diligent in all that he does. If he has a goal, he meets it *every single time*. Meanwhile, I'm on the struggle bus 90 percent of the time simply to complete my daily tasks. Although I joke about how this trait annoys me, it really is a wonderful trait to have.

I believe God wants us to be diligent women, too. Here are three ways to be diligent:

Be diligent in reading God's Word. It is what changes and transforms us. The Bible is God's perfect love letter written specifically for you. My husband once told me, "If you want to know what Jesus would say to you if He was standing right in front of you, read His Word; because that's exactly what He would talk about." It's true. Let's be women who are diligent about reading, studying, and memorizing this precious letter He has written to us.

Be diligent in prayer. Don't be the woman who just says the blessing and bedtime prayers with her kids. Be the woman who begins each day by talking to her Creator. He cares for you so much, and He wants you to talk to Him about every little detail of your life. The Bible tells us to pray without ceasing (1 Thessalonians 5:17). That simply means, talk to God all day, about everything. As women, we're already so good at talking, this should be easy. It doesn't have to be a weird thing, just talk.

Be diligent in serving at your local church. When you serve, whether it be as a greeter or rocking babies in the nursery (the real MVPs, who will have a special mansion in heaven), be diligent and serve with excellence. We all have a part to play in the church; find your part and do it well.

How will you be diligent this week?

DAY 12: SHE IS DILIGENT

Prayer

Jesus, thank You so much for Your precious love letter You have written to me. Help me to read the Bible with diligence and excitement. Thank You for dying on the cross so that I could be in direct conversation with God the Father all day, every day. Show me the area in my church where I can serve so that I can be a part of the community You've placed around me. In Jesus' name, amen.

SAY IT: *I am Diligent.*

READ IT: Proverbs 12:27, Proverbs 21:5, Galatians 6:9

WRITE IT: Start a journal and record your prayers each day for the next 30 days. PRO TIP: I did this for my husband for 30 days, and it made a precious gift for him.

day 13

She is Content

*"But Godliness with contentment is great gain.
For we brought nothing into the world, and we can take
nothing out, but if we have food and clothing, we will be content
with that. Those who want to get rich fall into temptation
and a trap and into many foolish and harmful desires that
plunge people into ruin and destruction."*

1 TIMOTHY 6:6-9

Can I take a moment to be brutally honest? It's very hard for me to look around at my life and just be thankful for what I have. I ride the struggle bus with this. I always want more—more for my kids, more for (or from) my husband, more for my house, more for my closet. As if this struggle isn't already real, then I take a gander at social media, where the epic Pinterest woman has already pinned and executed her board (insert eye roll), and somehow my beautiful life never measures up to the curated one. My husband shared a great quote with me recently that's so true: "Nothing destroys contentment like comparison." If we want to become the content woman God longs for us to be, we have got to stop comparing. Right now!

I have a sign hanging in my house that says "Live Simple." It's a great reminder to not get caught up in the latest and greatest. I'm not saying having nice things is bad; I'm just saying we must keep our motives in check. Are we coveting those shoes because all of our friends have them, or do we actually have an occasion to wear them? Are we considering a bigger house because we think we have something to prove, or do we simply need more room? Are we dreaming of vacationing in Italy because our Instagram feeds make it look inviting, or do we actually want to go there? We need to separate our real dreams and desires from the dreams and desires of others so that we can truly discover where we will find contentment.

If we're not careful, we will find our joy in things, not people. But what happens when those things go away? We then think our life has become an epic fail because we no longer measure up to this unrealistic standard we have placed on ourselves. Jesus longs for us to be content women who find our true contentment in a relationship with Him. We must be women who trust Him and live simply.

When we find true contentment in the ways of God, we're free to enjoy every season of life He has us in. Not just the seasons that bring us the good things (like new purses and shoes), but even the hard, ugly seasons that require lots of hot baths and therapy sessions. Contentment is simply saying, "Jesus, You have been so good to me, and if I never receive anything else from this world, what You have given me is more than enough."

Our time on earth is so valuable. Do we really want to spend it jealous and miserable? Let's choose contentment over comparison—today and every day.

Prayer

Father, help me to be content with this beautiful life You have given me. Help me to appreciate this day, even this very moment. Keep my eyes fixed on You and not on the people or things around me. You are so good to me. In Jesus' name, amen.

SAY IT: *I am Content.*

READ IT: 1 Timothy 6:6-9, Matthew 6:25-26, Hebrews 13:5

WRITE IT: Make a list of three things you can give away—that gift you got at your wedding that you've never used, jewelry you no longer wear, clothes that don't fit anymore, stuff that's been in your closet for years. Many times in my life, I have simply accumulated way too many things, but when I make a choice to declutter and create an atmosphere of giving, I find I'm able to understand and appreciate what a simple life really looks like.

day 14

She is Available

"Teach me your way O Lord; that I may rely on your faithfulness;
give me an undivided heart, that I may fear your name."

PSALM 86:11

The book you are reading right now would not exist if I didn't allow myself to be available. I knew God was birthing a book in me, but I gave Him every opportunity in the world to change His mind. (Yes, I realize how utterly ridiculous that sounds.) It seems no matter how many excuses I had for not writing a book, I would hear that still, small voice telling me to write. When I woke up, I heard it. When I went to sleep, I heard it. When I read books, I kid you not, they would say things like, "Has God called you to write a book?"

Believe me, I "started" so many times. I would make up my mind that this was the day I would begin and jot down some ideas, then BOOM, something unexpected would rattle me just enough for me to throw up my hands and say, "Nope, not today." The truth is with a husband who travels, two small children that I homeschool, and oh you know, just the everyday crazy of being a wife and mother, the "magical quiet moment" I was waiting for was never going to happen!

We will never have "time" to do something for God. We have to make a choice to simply be available. For months, I carried a notebook with me everywhere I went, and I physically wrote out my book with a pencil and paper. I finally decided I couldn't wait for a quiet moment with my laptop, my Bible, and a cup of coffee to start walking in my calling. It was in those brief moments, with pen and paper, where God gave me words; but I had to first make a choice to be available to Him in those moments.

Being available looks different for every woman. For you, it could mean that you get up before your circus begins, take time to read His Word and, for the love of all, have a hot cup of coffee. Being available might mean putting your phone down in that fifteen minutes of free time. Whatever it is that is stealing those little windows of precious time God gives you— even if it's in between pick-up lines, ballet lessons and dinner prep—make a choice today to do things that matter, things that will make a difference in your life and the lives of others. Every woman has a unique set of gifts to share with the world.

For me, it was writing a book to encourage women. So what if it took two years, right? I got it done…eventually; otherwise, we wouldn't be having this conversation. What has God called you to do? Be available today. Make room for Him to speak to you. Whatever He's telling you to do, don't put it off any longer. Other people's lives are waiting to be changed by what you have to give! Big or small, you never know what kind of impact your simple obedience to this one area can bring.

Prayer

Father, I pray I will allow myself to be available to You. No more excuses! Thank You for always pursuing me. You love me so much. Show me the plans You have for me. I pray I am obedient to You today. I want to be a part of changing lives for Your name's sake, and I know that starts with me saying, "I'm available, Lord." In the name of Your Son, I pray, amen.

SAY IT: *I am Available.*

READ IT: Psalm 86:11, Jeremiah 29:11

WRITE IT: Make a list of some ways you can make yourself more available to God. What is it for you? Earlier mornings? Less phone time? More time spent reading His Word? Starting a Bible study in your local church? Writing a book? In whatever ways God is leading you, make a choice today to be available.

She is Aware

"Watch and pray so that you will not fall into temptation. The spirit is willing but the flesh is weak."

MARK 14:38

What does it mean to be a woman who is aware? Many times we have our hearts, minds, and schedules so crowded, we can barely see two feet in front of us. We become so busy that we are constantly in "sink or swim" mode. Wait, did I just describe my life?

In the midst of the crazy, God is teaching me to simply be aware of Him. I would encourage you to ask Him to teach you this as well. Instead of waiting until Sunday to see if God shows up, look for Him in your everyday life. Be aware of Him when you are shopping and that amazing top you've been eyeing is on sale! (What?!?) Yes girl, that's God. The Bible says all good things come from Him. Sister, a sale is a GOOD thing, am I right? Be aware of Him in the busyness of life, especially in the little things, like your child's smile or a stranger's encouraging words.

Being aware of God means simply making a choice to press pause each day and say, "God, here I am. I want to make myself available to You. Help me, Jesus, to not miss You in any area of my life where You are speaking to me."

He's answered this prayer in my own life. In fact, one time I was encouraging a friend with the Scripture from Psalm 46:10: "Be still and know that I am God." I texted her the same Scripture probably four times in a week. Every time I would text her, I felt like I needed to hear it, too. I kept seeing this same verse pop up everywhere—on social media, in my favorite stores on paintings, even in my daily devotions.

That same week I found out my mom was going through some very difficult things. I was broken for her, and I wanted to rescue her and take away her heartache.God was telling me through this Scripture to trust Him and not fight battles that do not belong to me. He had my mom in His hands, and all I needed to do was to be still.

Finally, I bought a canvas that had the Scripture painted on it. I mean, it was meant to be, right? That Scripture has forever changed my life, because I chose to be aware of the Holy Spirit in every one of those moments. Had I not been looking for Jesus, I would have missed what He was trying to teach me.

Look around, and find God in the everyday. Be aware of

Jesus at home while you're sweeping the floor. Be aware of Him at the grocery store. Be aware of Him at your workplace or while you're spending time with your family or when you're driving in your car. He desires to spend time with His children, and His fingerprints are everywhere. Let's be women who openly receive His presence.

Prayer

Father, thank You so much for wanting me. Thank You, Jesus, for seeking me out on a daily basis. I pray I can find You in all that I do today—big or small. You are such a good, good Father. Help me to be aware of You today. I love you, Jesus. Amen.

SAY IT: *I am Aware.*

READ IT: Mark 14:38, Acts 17:28, Psalm 139:7-8

WRITE IT: Today, record all the little moments where God shows Himself to you. Those little moments can add up to big life change!

day 16

She is Chosen

"For he chose us in him before the creation of the world
to be holy and blameless in his sight. In love
he predestined us for adoption to sonship through Jesus,
in accordance with his pleasure and will."

EPHESIANS 1:4-5

When I hear the word *chosen*, it always takes me back to elementary PE class. Picture it: The coach chooses two captains. These two people (usually exceptional athletes) get to choose their teammates from a group of kids staring back at them, all hoping they get picked. Then the two teams play some kind of sport. It doesn't really matter which one, because I'm not good at any of them. I think to myself, "Maybe this time I won't be the last one chosen." But nope, once again, this stupid PE class leaves me feeling rejected, forcing me to be on a team where no one wants me.

The devil still makes us feel like that grade school girl,

doesn't he? He tells you no one wants you. No one *really* likes the real you; they only tolerate you. You start to tell yourself, "Everyone is better at everything than me." (By the way, be careful using words like *everyone* and *everything*. How could you possibly know that?)

When we start hearing these lies, it's important we recognize that the devil hates our guts. He wants nothing more than to destroy the fierce woman God is calling us to be. If he can make us feel unloved, less than, and unwanted, he has control over us; and he will hinder what God wants to do in our lives.

Paul, the writer of Ephesians, tells us God chose us before we even existed. He looked at you and me and said, "I want her. I want her to be my daughter. I am going to create her into a beautiful masterpiece, and then I am going to pursue her with an everlasting love. I know she will make mistakes. I know she will reject Me. I know she will fail; but none of that matters, because I am going to send my Son to die for her anyway. I CHOOSE her!" Yeah I know, that's a crazy love, right?!

The days will come when you feel overlooked. Sister, let this be a reminder to you that any feeling of not being wanted is of the devil. You, my friend, are loved, important, and chosen by the Creator of the universe. Ready to take on hell with a water pistol?! Yeah, me too! Let's go!

Prayer

God, I pray that I will receive the love You have given me today. Help me to walk in that love! I pray that I realize my worth and believe that You have chosen me even in my brokenness. You love me no matter what. You chose me then; You choose me now; and you will choose me tomorrow. I choose to receive that. In Jesus' name I pray, amen.

SAY IT: I *am Chosen.*

READ IT: Ephesians 1:4-5, Ephesians 2:10, 1 Peter 2:9

WRITE IT: Have there been moments in your life when you've felt *less than*? Maybe you feel that way right now. Journal about your feelings, and allow your Creator to wipe your tears, tear down the lies and help you believe what He says about you in His Word.

day 17

She is Joyful

"Nehemiah said, 'Go and enjoy choice food and sweet drinks, and send some to those who have nothing prepared. This day is holy to our Lord. Do not grieve, for the joy of the Lord is your strength.'"

NEHEMIAH 8:10

Author and theologian Henri Nouwen said, "Joy does not simply happen to us. We have to choose joy and keep choosing it every day." Wow, what a true statement. There is a difference in being happy and having joy. Happiness is based on *happenings*. When good things happen, you are happy. When bad things happen, you are sad. Joy, however, is an inner peace that remains steadfast through any circumstance.

I have a friend whom I often tease and tell her she is a modern-day Job. Anything that could go wrong, it's going to happen to her. She loves Jesus and always has complete trust in Him no matter what her circumstance says. She is the friend who stays positive in every situation. (Even though sometimes

75

I want to say, "Can we just be mopey today?") She once woke up to a flooded house. Now me, I would have flipped flat out in 2.5 seconds, but my friend turned on a worship song and held her husband's hand as they worshipped the Lord together standing in water up to their ankles. WHAT?! Yeah, I know. The only explanation for her behavior is that she has found true joy in her Savior. She has her mind made up that God is good, and no matter what her circumstance says, she will use it as a moment to find the good.

You and I are faced with the same choice every day. Do you look at what life gives you and sulk, or do you use it as a moment to allow God to fill you with joy? In order to receive His joy, we have to be in His Word. We have to unearth the peace He offers us. It's not enough for me to just tell you this, you have to discover it for yourself.

The Bible says, "*The joy of the Lord is our strength.*" That tells me joy can be a physical strength for us. Let's be women who chase joy down, grab it, and cling to it when life gets shaky. Let's be women other people look at and say, "How in the world is she so joyful in a circumstance like this?"

Prayer

Father, thank You for joy. Thank You that Your Word tells me Your joy is a strength for me when I am weak. You are so good to me. Help me to chase down the good. I receive Your joy today and make a choice right now to walk in it. In Jesus' name, amen.

SAY IT: *I am Joyful.*

READ IT: Nehemiah 8:10, Romans 15:13, James 1:2-3

WRITE IT: Nothing chases down joy like giving thanks. Make a list of all the things you are thankful for today, and praise God for those things.

day 18

She is Kind

*"Be kind and compassionate to one another, forgiving each other,
just as Christ forgave you."*
EPHESIANS 4:32

One of the most challenging movies I have ever seen is the movie *Wonder*. The film is about a boy with Treacher Collins syndrome. Born with rare facial deformities and no ears, this amazing little boy decides to go to a public school where he will inevitably be the laughing stock of his class. His bravery still gives me chills to this day. As you might suspect, because of the way he looks, he isn't treated with kindness. His mom had a saying that forever changed my life. She told her son, "In a world where you can be anything, be kind." I remind myself of this saying quite often any time I start getting frustrated with people for being too slow or not doing what I would like for them to do.

Like joy, kindness is a choice. It's also a gift we can all give, no matter our age, race, social status, job, or gender. God gives us opportunities all the time to give kindness away. Let's be women who have eyes to see opportunities to be kind!

I will never forget being in the grocery store all by myself one rare day—yes, I said it: ALL BY MYSELF (Thank you, Jesus!). I walked down every single aisle, slowly, paying attention to each detail and savoring the calm. When I was ready to check out, since I wasn't in a hurry, I meandered over to the first line I saw. I was intent on soaking up every second of this alone time.

Behind me, a frazzled lady with a screaming toddler looked like I usually do in the grocery store line with my kids. I turned around and insisted she go in front of me so she could get out of the store quicker. She was so grateful. She shared with me that she was from Texas. She and her daughter had been flying all day, and they were both exhausted. I didn't know her story beforehand; I just empathized with her situation. Of course, it was easy for me to show kindness in this moment because I was unusually relaxed and acutely aware of my surroundings. My prayer for myself and for you today is that we don't miss those opportunities where people need our kindness—even on our busiest days. In a world where you and I can be anything we want to be, may we choose to be kind.

Prayer

Jesus, thank You for being so kind to me. Thank You for giving me the perfect example of what kindness looks like. I pray You will give me opportunities to show kindness to people through my words, my smile and my actions. I choose kindness today. In Your name I pray, amen.

SAY IT: *I am Kind.*

READ IT: Ephesians 4:32, Acts 28:2, Romans 2:4

WRITE IT: Describe what kindness means to you. How has someone shown you kindness recently? How can you pay that kindness forward today?

day 19

She is Fearless

"For the spirit God gave us does not make us timid, but gives us power, love, and self-discipline."

2 TIMOTHY 1:7

A friend once told me, "Ivy, you've got to stop living in a 'what if' world." My first thought was, "Excuse me? I don't even say, 'What if' a lot." But as I started to examine my habits and the words I say on a daily basis, I realized, crap, she's right! On any given day I would say things like:

- "What if my son gets hurt doing that?"
- "What if my baby didn't eat enough?"
- "What if my husband wrecks driving home since he is so tired?"

The 'what ifs' would go on and on inside my fear-driven mind.

It's no secret that allowing fear to rule your mental and

spiritual life will greatly impact your physical life. Studies show fear weakens our immune system, impairs long-term memory, causes us to make impulsive decisions, and leads to depression. Fear is the body's natural way of responding to uncertainty, but it's our job to recognize the circumstances that trigger fear for us. These triggers can look different for everyone.

Once I acknowledged it was fear that was driving my decisions and causing anxiety, I was able to combat that fear with faith. I had to call those fears out for what they were—lies. I don't know what fears you have today, but what I do know is we serve a God who turns fear into a faith that is unstoppable.

Studies have shown that there are certain sound waves that are only stopped by producing the exact opposite sound wave, which silences the original sound. I believe the same is true with fear. We must memorize Scriptures that are the complete opposite of the lies the devil feeds us—Scriptures filled with truth. Here are a few examples:

Isaiah 41:10
"So do not fear, for I am with you; do not be dismayed, for I am your God. I will strengthen you and help you; I will uphold you with my righteous right hand."

Psalm 56:3
"When I am afraid, I put my trust in you."

1 John 4:18

"There is no fear in love. But perfect love drives out fear, because fear has to do with punishment. The one who fears is not made perfect in love."

Proverbs 12:25

"Anxiety weighs down the heart, but a kind word cheers it up."

Fear is one of the most powerful weapons the enemy uses against women. Worry and anxiety can keep our minds distracted from a God who desires for us to completely trust Him. I believe our Creator is wise to the enemy, and that's why He gave us 365 Bibles verses on fear. Think about it. How many days are in a year? Yes, 365! A Scripture for every day! Friends, isn't our God so good to us? For daughters of the King, there is *nothing* to fear.

Prayer

Father, help me to realize when fear is creeping at my door.
Give me the strength to not let it come in. Help me to remember
Your Word so that I can counteract the enemy's lies.
No matter what circumstances come my way, I have full
confidence that You are in control. I will replace fear with faith.
In Jesus' powerful name I pray, amen.

SAY IT: *I am Fearless.*

READ IT: Isaiah 41:10, 2 Timothy 1:7

WRITE IT: Once you find some key Scriptures that help you replace fear with faith, write those down. Then place them in spots where you can see them every day as a reminder of the God you serve.

day 20

She is Worthy

"'For I know the plans I have for you,' declares the Lord. '
Plans to prosper you and not to harm you.
Plans to give you a hope and a future.'"

JEREMIAH 29:11

I haven't always felt worthy enough to be used by God. It's something I have struggled with for a long time. I don't have any known talents, and I often lack discipline. Most of the time, I feel like I'm just an average house wife trying not to mess my kids up. I spent years believing these lies, fearing I would never amount to anything.

However, as I began to uncover the truth found in God's Word, it was only then that I started to recognize my worth. I began to see that I was created by God and for God. I started to believe He has given me special gifts and talents to be used to glorify His name.

Time and time again, as I read the Bible, God spoke to my

heart, "Ivy, know who you are and know that that is enough." Slowly, I'm beginning to understand that God is so in love with me. He pursues me every single day. Nothing I have done, do, or will do makes me worthy. He calls me worthy because of His Son's finished work on the cross. Sister, God feels the exact same way about you. He wants you to know He sees you; He values you, and He loves you. If I could only look you in the eyes in this moment, I would tell you, "You matter. You are worthy. You are enough."

The enemy recognizes our tendencies to feel unworthy. When the devil steals our worth, it gives us permission to walk without purpose. But sister, let me tell you:

When you think, "No one loves me." God says, "I do, and I'll never stop."

When you think, "I'll never do anything significant for the Kingdom." God says, "You can do all things through Christ who gives you strength."

When you think, "I'm not pretty enough or smart enough." God says, "You are fearfully and wonderfully made."

Friend, you are worthy simply because God says you are. And that is enough. You no longer have permission to walk without purpose.

Prayer

Lord, thank You for giving me worth. Thank you for sending Jesus to die for me and for loving me through my mess. Thank You for telling me truth when the world tells me lies. In moments of sadness and loneliness, remind me that I am worthy because You say I am. Amen.

SAY IT: *I am Worthy.*

READ IT: Jeremiah 29:11, John 3:16, Ephesians 2:10

WRITE IT: Who are you? Write a description of who you are below. For example, mine would say: *I am a daughter of the King of Kings. I am the wife of Noah Cleveland. I am a mother to two amazing boys and will be a mother to more children in the future. I am a friend. I am a daughter. I am a sister.* (Writing out who we are helps us realize just how valuable we are.)

She is Compassionate

*"Therefore as God's chosen people, holy and dearly loved, c
lothe yourselves with compassion, kindness,
humility, gentleness, and patience."*
Colossians 3:12

I am an "action = consequence" type of girl. I believe you
do A, and you will reap B. You get the picture. There have been
so many times in my life when I have been quick to say, "Well,
they should have listened." Believe me, I say this to myself, too,
every time I step on a scale and recognize the consequences of
poor eating habits as a higher number appears on this device
from the pits of hell.

I am so grateful Jesus doesn't look at me that way. He,
instead, looks at every one of His daughters and says, "Yes,
I know what you have done. Yes, I see your sin; but I love
and forgive you anyway." He has great compassion on us and
encourages us to freely extend compassion to others.

She is...

Let me make one thing clear. Having compassion on people doesn't give them a free pass to use you. There are still boundaries we must put in place—even as we seek to love like Jesus. The key to this is simple. We must follow the Holy Spirit's leading. In fact, I think compassion is one way in which the Holy Spirit speaks.

I'm not saying it's your Christian duty to help every homeless person you see or to give someone in need all your mortgage money. What I am saying is when the Holy Spirit leads you to help someone, look upon them with the compassion of Jesus, and do whatever He tells you to do. Compassion can be such a gift! Compassion can lead us to pray for people in a way we haven't before, because compassion helps us look at the person suffering, not just the cause of their suffering.

So many times in the Bible, it tells us that before Jesus healed someone He would look on them with compassion. *Then* the miracle would take place. Perhaps you and I need to adjust our focus. Perhaps we need to extend compassion and make way for miracles. Let's be women who live with compassion in our eyes, always leading people to the cross of Jesus even in the midst of their mess.

Prayer

Father, thank You for loving me enough not to look at my sin and turn away. Thank You that, instead, You look at my sin and draw close to me. Today, help me to have compassion in my eyes, in my hands, in my heart, and in my spirit. Lord, I pray I can love people the way You do. In Jesus' name, amen.

SAY IT: *I am Compassionate.*

READ IT: Colossians 3:12, Matthew 9:35-38, Matthew 14:14

WRITE IT: Make a list of people you have a hard time feeling compassion toward. I want you to spend the next seven days praying for these people. Be diligent about this; don't miss a day. Ask God to change your heart toward these people and to give you eyes to see them as the face of God.

day 22

She is Secure

"Charm is deceptive, beauty is fleeting; but a woman who fears the Lord is to be praised."

PROVERBS 31:30

I read a quote once that said, "Nothing is more impressive than a woman who is secure in the unique way God made her." I have been married to my bookie for 12 years now, and I can say with full certainty I have made it quite interesting for him. There have been days he had no idea "who" he was coming home to. (Insert the laughing emoji here. By the way, writing without using emojis is extremely difficult.)

Recently, the Lord really began to deal with my insecurities. Some days I'm so confident in who I am as a wife, friend, and mom; and then there are days when… Well, let's just say they aren't my finest moments.

My husband travels full-time for a living leading worship all across the country. Most of the time, the boys and I go with him, but there are still more than a handful of times that we don't. Can I just be vulnerable here and tell you how my "not so great moments" look?

Without fail, every time my husband travels without us, the devil wreaks havoc on my mind:

You're not the wife you think you are.

He's probably connecting with a female worship leader right now, who fully understands the music world—the world you have no clue about.

Just look at your kids! You haven't even cooked them a meal since he's been gone. They have eaten cheeseburgers and chicken nuggets every day.

Your husband doesn't fully understand you and all that you have been through.

Y'all. It. Gets. Brutal.

The more insecure I feel, the more I look to Noah to make me feel secure. How do I do that, you ask? I send him back-to-back text messages and only call him about five hundred times. (No big deal, really.) I *need* to feel needed by him. Surely, if he sees how weak I am, he will be my knight in shining armor, rushing in to save his princess.

Can I just tell you something? This never works. It actually has the opposite effect. The more I push, the more he pulls away. I've learned he needs to stay sane so that he can lead people to Jesus in the places he's sent. I mean, who does he think he is, leaving me alone with my thoughts? All for what? To change people's destinies from death to life? I know, I know, you're thinking to yourself, "*Wow, what a nut case!*" I am not going to disagree with you. However, can I just tell you, I am not who I once was! Feel better? Can we be friends again?

I'm thankful my husband does not enable this way of thinking. It forces me to go to Jesus to sort this mess out. What I always discover is that I need to find my security in my Maker, not my husband. Noah will always let me down, even on his best day, simply because he was not created to make me feel secure. I understand this is not what the world tells us; but I promise you if you look to a person, place, or thing to make you feel secure, you will be let down every single time.

There is nothing attractive about a weak woman who has no idea who she is. If you want to get your man's attention, get in God's Word, find out who you are and walk in that security. That, my friends, is the beginning of true beauty.

FYI, no one was hurt during my emotional breakdowns.

Prayer

Father in heaven, I need You to comfort me. I need You to settle this knot in my stomach that is telling me I need to be needed. I pray right now You would flood me with your peace and love so that I can be secure in You. Show me in Your Word who You say I am and help me to walk in that. Amen.

SAY IT: *I am Secure.*

READ IT: Romans 8:38-39, 2 Thessalonians 3:3

WRITE IT: Find a piece of paper (preferably a cute one, because that totally makes the note more legit), and write down your insecurities. Then, beside each insecurity, write out a Scripture verse to combat those feelings.

day 23

She is Blessed

"You will be blessed when you come in and blessed when you go out."

DEUTERONOMY 28:6

As women, we tend to focus on things we don't have. Like the times I want to get my nails done. My nails say, "Oh girl, look at those cuticles!" But my bank account says, "Didn't you just say you needed new jeans?" We can always look at our life and see something we feel we're lacking; but the truth is, if we have air in our lungs, a roof over our head, clothes on our body, and food on our table, we are blessed women with a capital B.

As a mother, I love when my boys thank me for things. I love them knowing how good they have it. I love hearing them give genuine thanks for their life. Now they don't realize that's what they're doing. In their minds, they're just saying those two words I have threatened they better say when given something. (Did I say *threatened*? I meant *strongly encouraged.*)

Shouldn't we make a habit of telling our Father in heaven "thank you" for the many blessings He has given to us? Don't you think He wants to hear His kids say things like, "Thank You, Father, for my house, my kids, my husband, my job, my vehicle, etc."? The list could go on and on of things we see and use every single day that we could thank Him for. Often, we just come to expect these things, but make no mistake, we have what we have because our Father has gifted these things to us.

The Bible tells us in Deuteronomy, when we obey God, He will bless us abundantly. God is so good to us. He only wants good for us. Let's give Him thanks for that.

I understand we all have hard days when we wonder, *Where are the blessings of God?* The truth is, not every day will be good, but there is good in every day. Seek it out, and give Him thanks for it. There are times in my life where I just have a negative attitude about any and every thing. There is no beauty in that. When I realize this is happening, I will go on what I like to call a "negative fast." I make a choice to stop with the negativity. Even if I feel entitled to my negativity, I will only speak positivity for a few days just to get my mind refocused on the goodness of God.

You and I are too blessed to allow the devil to tell us what we "don't have." If God doesn't do anything else for us the rest of our lives here on earth, Him saving us from the pit of hell

DAY 23: SHE IS BLESSED

is more than enough! He gave us eternal life, ya'll! We are too blessed to be stressing about things that don't matter.

Prayer

God, I just want to say thank You so much for who You are.
Thank You, sweet Jesus, that You have given me life.
Thank You that You have blessed my life so abundantly.
So many times I overlook the blessings in my life. God, help me to
see the many blessings around me today and to give You praise
for every single one. In Jesus' name, amen.

SAY IT: *I am Blessed.*

READ IT: John 1:16, Philippians 4:19, James 1:17

WRITE IT: Write those blessings out, girl! Don't you skip a single one!

day 24

She is Courageous

"Have I not commanded you? Be strong and courageous.
Do not be afraid. Do not be discouraged, for the Lord your God
will be with you wherever you go."

JOSHUA 1:9

Sometimes (well, a lot of times), God calls us to things that are much bigger than we are to show us His power. God knows us far better than we know ourselves, and He knows what we are capable of. He knows our areas of strength and our areas of weakness.

The truth is, it takes courage to fulfill God's call on your life. Don't you dare back down from what God has called you to do just because you don't understand the full outcome of the plan. I know, for me and my life, that has been one of the biggest roadblocks. Years ago, I knew God was calling me to something new, but I didn't understand how it would work. So instead of being brave and pressing in, I allowed fear to dictate my path. The problem is fear holds you back every time.

Courage, on the other hand, says, "I am in this for the long haul." Courage says, "I may see things fall to my left and to my right, but I trust that God has a plan that will prevail." Ladies, courage is putting your big girl panties on, pulling your hair in a ponytail, and slaying your day.

After I had my second son, I felt the Holy Spirit leading me to quit my job so I could stay home with my babies. I knew God was leading me to give up a career that I enjoyed to make myself available to travel full-time with my husband and homeschool our boys. I fought His leading tooth and nail. Me, a stay-at-home mom? What?! A teacher? *This cannot possibly be from God*, I thought.

Without fail, God continued to gently pursue me. He used people I knew to confirm this decision, as well as complete strangers. Aren't you so thankful we serve a God who is patient enough with us to continue to chase us down? After countless affirmations, I finally knew this was indeed something God Himself was leading me to do. So I stepped out in faith, quit my job, and made the leap to be a SAHM.

Can I tell you a secret? It has not always been easy. Even though I know without a shadow of doubt that we are right in the middle of God's will, there are still days I think to myself, *Ivy, you could still be working, and there is an elementary school not even a mile from your house!* I've even had numerous people tell me how hard it is on my boys for us to keep them on the road all the time, making me second-guess my decision.

(Do people really think saying things like that is encouraging?) Regardless of the opinions of others, the truth remains. We did not fall into this calling by chance. God ordained it; so He will sustain us in order for His purposes to be accomplished.

So, sister, let me be your motivational coach today! Get up, and take courage. Fight for what God has called you to do. You are not weak. You were created to be a stinkin' warrior girl! (BTW go check out my book, *Warrior Girl*. I know it will inspire you to be strong when the struggle is real) Today, choose to fight like the warrior princess you are!

 *Prayer*

God, thank You so much for the courageous spirit You have given me. I pray today I can unlock courage through Your Word. Give me courage like you gave so many people in the Bible who faced impossible situations. I know You are for me and that with You, there is nothing I cannot do. Thank You for making me a warrior. In Jesus' name, amen.

SAY IT: *I am Courageous.*

READ IT: Joshua 1:9, Deuteronomy 31:8, 1 Corinthians 16:13

WRITE IT: Has there been an instance in your life that required great courage? Can you look back now and see how God brought you through that time? Write down the story of that experience, and relive that moment where God made a way for you and gave you supernatural strength.

day 25

She is Victorious

"For the Lord your God is the one who goes with you to fight for you against your enemies to give you victory."
Deuteronomy 20:4

$\mathcal{M}$y grandmother was a sweet lady. She always had a piece of Big Red chewing gum ready to give you. She loved going to church. Although her love for Jesus shined through, it always left me confused to see her with such a defeated spirit. She would be smiling one minute, and then the second you asked her, "How are you doing today?" her smile quickly turned to a frown. She would begin to tell you all the negativity she was feeling. It was as if all the air got sucked out of the room in that moment. This happened every single time without fail.

As Christ followers, we have no reason to live in defeat. People should be drawn to us because they feel strength, confidence, and hope when they are around us. They should never feel the urge to take one look at us and run for cover.

Don't get a reputation as a Negative Nancy. (No offense to anyone named Nancy.)

Everyone experiences defeat from time to time, but that doesn't mean we have to wallow in it. I, myself, have experienced great defeat in my life. One morning I woke up to my baby crying from his crib in the other room. I got out of bed and fell straight to the ground. My feet were no longer working! My baby was still crying, so I crawled to his room. I grabbed hold of his crib and pulled myself up. Using all the upper body strength I could muster, I was able to pick my baby up, and then I collapsed with him in my arms right there in front of the crib. I had no idea what was going on! I was later diagnosed with psoriatic arthritis. My joints were so inflamed, they simply would not move.

I felt so defeated during this season of life. I spent months praying that God would heal my body. I believed with all my heart that He would. I knew He was capable of this. I had seen Him do it in the lives of my friends! But here I was in a desperate time of need, and yet, I felt so alone and scared. I knew I needed my Father to give me supernatural strength to endure this. So I clung to Him. I clung to His Word, and I learned a very important lesson. Our victory does not come from any circumstance; it comes through God's Word. Real victory is knowing who you are in Jesus Christ no matter what happens in your life. That's how you can hold onto hope during hard situations.

Focus on the good, friend! Always find a reason to praise His name! That's true victory! Your circumstances may not change, but one thing I guarantee will change is your perspective. Let me tell you, sweet friend, a change in perspective is everything. The right perspective will bring victory in your life. Even on our toughest days, we can have victory in Christ when we realize He is working all things together for the good of those who love Him. Amen?

Prayer

God, thank You for who You are. Thank You that I can take You at Your Word and know that You only want what's best for me. Thank You for victory through You. I pray today You would change my perspective. Even on days that are not good, help me to find the good in every day! In the name of Your son I pray, amen.

SAY IT: *I am Victorious.*

READ IT: Deuteronomy 20:4, Romans 8:37

WRITE IT: Make a list of the things you are seeking victory over. Ask the Lord to show you your next step. Perhaps you just need a new perspective, or maybe there is a physical action you need to take to gain victory over your circumstance. Part of what brought healing to my body was cutting out gluten, taking medication, and exercising. Maybe there is something hindering you from walking in the victory God has called you to walk in.

day 26

She is Peaceful

"Peace I leave with you, my peace I give you. I do not give to you as the world gives to you. Do not let your hearts be troubled and do not be afraid."

JOHN 14:27

The devil tries to steal our peace daily. It's one of his greatest tactics. If he can rob us of the peace Jesus offers, then it will cause a trickle effect of unraveling in every area of our lives.

Are you wondering if your peace is being snatched from you? Examine how you handle situations that are challenging. How do you respond to bad news? How do you handle the curve balls life throws at you? Do you practice patience when things don't go your way? Are you stressed or anxious all the time?

In the Scripture above, notice that Jesus says He *gives* us peace. If someone gives you something, it is your choice whether or not to take it. Peace is something we have to receive from Jesus daily. We have to make a choice to accept His gift and own it!

If we're really honest, allowing our peace to be stolen is ultimately a way of saying, "God, I don't trust You." When our trust is in our Creator, peace reigns in our hearts regardless of our circumstances. We are able to trust that if God is for us, then who (or what) can stand against us?

There have been many times in my life where I've felt like everything was going smoothly, and I was at peace; then, all of a sudden—*bam!* Just like a thief in the night, the devil robs me of my peace. I start feeling anxious and asking a series of "what if" questions. In those moments, you and I have to cling to what we know is true. We have to cling to Jesus and what His Word tells us about His character. We have to trust the peace only He can give.

Don't let the devil steal your peace. In fact, don't let him steal anything that Jesus says is yours to keep!

Prayer

God, You are so good to me. Thank You for being the Prince of Peace. Thank You that You offer a real peace that surpasses all understanding. I pray today that I may receive that peace and own it. No matter what this day brings, help me, Lord, to cling to You. Help me to cling to what I know is true. You are the author of peace, and I thank You for sharing that gift with me. In Jesus' name, amen.

SAY IT: *I am Peaceful.*

READ IT: John 14:27, Romans 8:31, Colossians 3:15,

WRITE IT: What is robbing you of peace? Is it one thing? Is it ten things? Whatever it is, you must acknowledge it and call it out. We can't change what we don't acknowledge. Write down all the things, then I want you to take a match to it. Now, don't get all pyromaniac on me. Just a small (controlled!) fire will do. This is simply symbolic that the devil doesn't own you. You have the right to possess the peace that Jesus provides.

day 27

She is Loved

*"For God so loved the world that he gave his one
and only son, that whoever believes in him
shall not perish but have everlasting life."*

JOHN 3:16

As women, we are all created differently, but there is one thing that remains true of all of us: We want to feel like the most loved girl on the planet! We seek love all day long from our husbands, children, friends, and family members. Feeling loved is usually at the top of my list every day, even if I don't want to admit it. I often ask my boys, "What do you love about Mom?" My husband rolls his eyes, because he knows what's happening in this moment. But hey, I just want to feel the love… No shame in my game.

When the people we are closest to fail to fulfill this huge burden we place on them, we are left feeling broken. The devil loves for you and I to feel this way. He wants us to walk in defeat. Feeling unloved and unwanted can certainly do that to a girl.

For years I thought no one understood the "real me"—not even my husband. He didn't understand what I needed, because he clearly wasn't giving it to me. He didn't understand that I needed to hear that I was not just pretty, but *hot*. I wanted to feel like he wanted me. He didn't understand that I needed him to listen to the details of my day. I needed to feel heard and known. He didn't understand that I wanted him to be the one chasing me instead of me hounding him like a gnat at a picnic. The problem, though, wasn't with Noah; the problem was with me.

It was a great revelation (and relief!) when I realized Noah was never meant to complete me. He was never going to make me feel loved in all the ways I craved. I had to seek my Father in heaven for this type of all-encompassing love. When I began to allow God to show me just how much He truly loves and cares for me, I became less needy. Truth be told, I wish I hadn't spent so many years putting so many unrealistic expectations on my husband.

John 3:16 tells us God loved us so much that He sent His only Son to a world to be beaten, mocked, and crucified just to be in relationship with us, just to show us how much He loves us. Wow! That truth brings a whole new meaning to the word love, doesn't it?

Princess Diana was once quoted as saying, "The biggest

disease in this day and age is that of people feeling unloved." This statement is so true. Sister, God has not called us to live a life of defeat. He has called us to live a life of full joy, full peace, and full security.

If you want to love people with the fullness of God, then you must receive His love for you first. Understand it. Crave it. Seek it. Own it. He loves you, sister, with a love that cannot be replicated or manufactured. He loves you with the purest love that has the ability to transform you from the inside out. Friend, let the love of Jesus fill every longing in your heart today!

Prayer

Sweet Jesus, thank You so much for loving me enough to die for me. Thank You that I am never alone because You are always with me. Thank You, Jesus, for Your goodness in my life. Thank You for making me feel loved today. I love you, Lord. Amen.

SAY IT: *I am Loved.*

READ IT: Psalm 36:7, John 3:16, Romans 5:8,

WRITE IT: Write out some of the Scriptures that remind you how much God loves you. When I really want my sons to learn something in school, I make them write it out. On days you feel unloved, quote these Scriptures out loud, and know that you are never alone.

day 28

She is Brave

*"Do not be anxious about anything, but in
every situation, by prayer and petition, with thanksgiving,
present you requests to God."*

PHILIPPIANS 4:6-7

I have always wanted to be a real-life Disney princess! I
love movies like *Cinderella*, *Beauty and the Beast*, and *Snow
White*—you know, all the movies with the classic princesses.
But recently, there is a new Disney princess that defeats all the
odds! She's a frizzy red-headed warrior named Merida, and she
is not afraid of anything. She is fierce.

Don't you want people to think of you that way? I do! I
want people to look at me and say, "Wow! She is a force to be
reckoned with!" In order to become this warrior of a woman,
we must be brave. We must look at the situation in front of us
and know the same God that rose from the grave lives inside
us; and we can conquer anything!

The Bible tells us not to be anxious about anything. It doesn't say, "You can be anxious about a few things." I mean really, though, how do we become women who live like that?!

Can I be honest with you for a split second? This is so hard for me! I put the 'A' in anxious. Then God tells me that I'm not to be anxious about anything?! Are you kidding me?

There is hope though, ladies! If I can grab hold of this truth, so can you. We must be grounded in God's Word. That is the only way to be brave enough to let our anxious feelings float away. Being brave doesn't mean we will never experience fear or doubt. It just means pressing on anyway. Speaking Scripture over our circumstances helps. Scripture like:

1 John 4:4
"Greater is He who lives in me than He who lives in the world."

Romans 8:37
"I am more than a conquerer."

Philippians 4:13
"I can do all things through Christ who gives me strength."

Above all, remember this: You are never alone. Jesus lives within you. When you are in a room, so is He. When you are in your car, so is He. When you are at work, so is He. He is always with you! You are never a party of one, but always a party of two. Be bold; be beautiful; be brave!

Prayer

God, thank You for Your power at work in me. Thank You, Jesus, that You live inside of me. Thank You that I am never alone. Thank You for giving me Scripture to use in my life against my fear, worry, and anxiety. You give me strength to be brave, bold, and fearless. Help me to own that today. In Jesus' name, amen.

SAY IT: *I am Brave.*

READ IT: Philippians 4:6-7, Deuteronomy 31:6-8

WRITE IT: Write down some Scripture verses below that make you brave. You already know why! When we write it, we remember it. When we remember it, we say it.

day 29

She is Fun

"So I command the enjoyment of life, because there is nothing better for a person under the sun than to eat and drink and be glad. Then joy will accompany them in their toil all the days of their life God has given them under the sun."

ECCLESIASTES 8:15

At times I can be a drill sergeant, especially with my kids. As women, we are always (x100) in "go" mode. We have a thousand and one tasks to accomplish on a daily basis. If you have children, this is where I would add that along with all the tasks we mamas have, we also have to keep tiny humans alive. If you are a wife and a mom, you have to do all the above, plus show adequate attention to your husband. Ahhh... I am exhausted just thinking about all that!

Sisters, God does not want us to dread everyday life. We can either be miserable, or we can choose to have fun every single day. I say we choose to live in the moment—even the moments we feel we're "too busy" to enjoy. Of course, there are things that need to be done throughout the day, but let's be women who are intentional about remaining fun.

I recently had a rare day where I thought I was running ahead. You know what I mean…dishes washed; dinner going in the crock pot; floors vacuumed; laundry clean, dried, and folded; beds made, etc. Then I came around the corner to find my boys had taken my couch cushions off the couch and created a slide going down our staircase. Now, every fiber of my being wanted to go full-on drill sergeant on them in that moment! Instead, I had to remember to just be fun! So you know what I did? I went down that cushion slide!

My boys absolutely loved me dialing back the intensity for just a moment and being present with them. As busy women, we have to give ourselves permission to have fun for no other reason than to simply enjoy life. I have heard it said, "Laughter is medicine to the soul." It's so true! Choose today to just be fun.

You may be asking yourself, "What does being fun have to do with the way God sees me?" Well, as you read in Ecclesiastes, you'll see that King Solomon, who was the wisest king who ever lived, suggested that the way to happiness is to eat, drink and be glad (aka: Have fun with your life!). Friends, God desires fun for us. Don't miss out on the fun that can be found in the most ordinary moments!

Prayer

God, thank You for wanting me to enjoy my life. Thank You that it's OK to have fun. I pray today that I can be that woman. When people look at me, I pray they see joy that flows from the inside out. Help me to chase down moments that allow me to simply have fun. In Your name I pray, amen.

SAY IT: *I am Fun.*

READ IT: Ecclesiastes 8:15

WRITE IT: Make a list of ways you can be fun. Be intentional, and start making room for fun every single day!

day 30

She is Discerning

*"And this I pray, that your love may abound still more
and more in real knowledge and all discernment, so that you may
approve the things that are excellent, in order to be sincere and
blameless until the day of Christ."*

PHILIPPIANS 1:9-10

Women's intuition is real, ya'll. To be discerning women, we must know how to recognize the truth. We have to have enough of God's Word deposited in us, so that when questions, concerns, or gray areas arise, we will be able to lean on that truth. The truth will then lead us in the right direction.

Sometimes God will even use your keen sense of discernment to help your husband. Case in point, there was a time Noah had a female wanting to become his booking agent. My husband is an amazing worship leader, so it isn't uncommon for people to seek him out wanting to book him for events. When I met this particular lady for the first time, I did not have peace about her. I couldn't pinpoint exactly what it was that made me uneasy, but there was just something in my spirit that wasn't clicking with her.

Noah, on the other hand, didn't pick up on any weird vibes from this woman. So he had to trust my discernment alone (No pressure!). This lady ended up coming to an event where Noah was leading worship. Afterwards, she asked him to come to a back room with her. (Calm down! He didn't do it!) He said, "Sure, but let me grab my wife real quick." (Proud wife moment!) I went with him to the back room, and it was super awkward. You could tell she didn't have anything to say once we were both in there. Shortly afterwards, she vanished. We have no clue where she is to this day.

I couldn't tell you exactly what her motives were or what my "feeling" was other than I know it was discernment from the Holy Spirit telling me to protect my husband. Listen, there are going to be times when you will discern something that no one else will see, but that's OK. Trust God, and be obedient.

That doesn't give us license to abuse this special gift of discernment; but instead, we should follow it and let it speak for itself. I never had to force my husband to listen to me when it came to that lady. He trusted my discernment because it's proven to be true so many times throughout our marriage—a marriage built on trust.

A word of warning here, ladies. Just like with anything else, the devil can use your intuition against you. As wise women, we have to make sure our "feeling" isn't based on jealously or bitterness. (Been there, done that, got the T-shirt. Just take my word for it— you don't want it.) Before voicing our concerns, we need to seek the Lord and ask Him to clarify our discernment.

In order to grow in this gift, it's crucial that we spend time with Jesus and meditate on His Word. This will help us to know when it's the Holy Spirit leading us, versus our flesh leading us. This can get tricky at times, but if we practice hearing God's truth, it makes it a littler easier to discern His voice.

Prayer

God, I pray for my gift of discernment. I pray You would help me use discernment today to recognize unhealthy relationships in my own life and in the lives of those closest to me.

Help me to see which relationships are toxic and which relationships are valuable. Help me to practice listening to You so that I know when it's Your voice speaking versus my flesh speaking. In Jesus' name, amen.

SAY IT: *I am Discerning.*

READ IT: Philippians 1:9-10

WRITE IT: Are there any relationships you are uneasy about? Write them down, and commit to praying about them. Ask God to show you in a real way if this is the Holy Spirit or if this is your flesh speaking to you.

day 31

She is Wise

"Blessed are those who find wisdom, those who gain understanding. For she is more profitable than silver and yields better return than gold. She is more precious than rubies; nothing you desire can compare to her."

PROVERBS 3:13-15

When I was 16 years old, I met a lady at church who was three times my age. She taught me so much about life, how to pray, and how to believe God for the impossible. She taught me that God cared for me as His daughter and that I could put my full trust in Him. She helped me understand that He would take care of me no matter what. It was this sweet lady's time and wisdom that helped mold me into the woman I am today.

To become wise women, we have to find other women who are ahead of us in the journey. Women who are chasing after God and live their lives according to the Bible. Women who are willing to spend time passing their wisdom down to us.

In turn, we must put in the work. We must pursue wisdom. Chase it down even. Wisdom is not just given to us because we merely wake up every morning. We have to intentionally seek it out.

Let's be women who seek wisdom from God's Word. Let's be women who seek wisdom from other women. Let's be women who seek wisdom from sermons, books, and podcasts. Let's be women who seek wisdom from life experiences. Let's be women who remain teachable. I love that God gives us so many smart women in Scripture from which to glean wisdom. I think back to strong women like Ruth, who trusted God with her very life, even though she didn't know how it would end. Knowing her story allows me to learn from it and apply it to my own life.

As women, we often think we already know it all and don't need any help; but you know what I have come to realize? I don't actually know it all! Shocking, right? I crave wisdom, and I believe you should, too. Let's be women who are always ready to listen and always willing to learn. I promise you, if you're willing to look for her, there's an older woman a few steps ahead of you just waiting to be your friend. Get in God's Word, find a mentor, and stay close to God in prayer. I promise, He will shape you into a wise woman!

Prayer

*Lord Jesus, thank You so much for placing the Word in my life
to give me wisdom. Thank You for allowing me to draw wisdom
from life experience. Thank You for putting other women in my
life to mentor me. I pray I do not miss one opportunity to learn.
Help me to be open-minded to what You want to do in my life.
In the name of Your Son I pray, amen.*

SAY IT: *I am Wise.*

READ IT: Proverbs 3:13-18

WRITE IT: Write down the names of a few Godly women
who are older and wiser than you. Schedule time to spend with
them, and let them pour into your life.

day 32

She is Fruitful

"You did not choose me, but I chose you and appointed you so that you might go and bear fruit—fruit that will last. And so that whatever you ask in my name, the father will give you."

JOHN 15:16

When we become born-again believers, it doesn't just stop there. Salvation is simply the first step on our faith journey. God has called us to a life that produces good fruit. Consider this: If an apple tree is thriving at its roots, it is going to bring forth a delicious fruit that has many benefits for your body. If the tree is dead at its roots, it will produce nothing at harvest time.

As Christians, it is so important to plant our roots in the right soil. Here are three things I think will help us produce Godly fruit:

1. First and foremost, we need to be rooted in the Word. If we are going to be women who bear fruit for the Kingdom,

135

we have to know about the Kingdom. Just as you study for a test, you must study the Word. Read it, memorize it, and know it so that when the tests of life come, you'll be ready to ace them.

2. The second thing that brings forth lasting fruit is a group of other women of faith to walk alongside you. My life forever changed when I joined a women's Sunday School class at my church. These women challenge me, love me, serve me, and speak life over me. They call out bad seeds growing in me before they ever come to fruition.

3. The last way in which we can be women who produce good fruit is to serve. Cultivate a servant's heart. Volunteer in a needed area at your local church, or serve your husband in an unexpected way. Maybe you could help a mama in need! (I'm always in need of this!) When we serve other people, it causes us to die to ourselves, and in return, creates a giving spirit within us. A giving spirit is very fruitful for the Kingdom.

The Bible tells us in Galatians the Fruits of the Spirit are love, joy, peace, forbearance, kindness, goodness, faithfulness, gentleness, and self-control. Now, there are days that I just flat out stink at most of these; but these are the sweet things God wants to grow in us. To be a fruitful woman of faith and produce the Fruits of the Spirit, we must be grounded in His Word, surrounded by a community of believers, and involved in service to others.

Prayer

Lord Jesus, thank You for choosing me. You care about every detail of my life and want me to grow in You. Lord, I pray when I read Your Word, I will let it transform me. Help me build a community around me to challenge me. Show me areas in my life where I can serve others. In Jesus' name, amen.

SAY IT: *I am Fruitful.*

READ IT: John 15:16

WRITE IT: Write down the nine fruits the Bible tells us we should have. Go through each one and ask God to teach you how to grow in these areas. (Buckle up buttercup, it might get crazy!)

day 33

She is Encouraging

"Therefore encourage one another and build each other up, just in fact as you are doing."

1 Thessalonians 5:11

I went through a hard season a few years ago. I had a newborn, a toddler, a traveling husband, and a crippling, incurable disease called psoriatic arthritis. It was rough. On any given day, I didn't know whether I was coming or going. My newborn had colic and severe acid reflux. My toddler had more energy than the Energizer Bunny on steroids. All the moms reading this know exactly what I mean when I say I lived on Jesus and coffee. Amen?!

Some days were better than others, but there was one particular day that I'm pretty sure I prayed for Jesus to return. I had hit my limit. Just like any other day, I checked the mail, and there was a precious, unexpected gift inside. A friend I hadn't seen in a while sent me a necklace that had the words

"Be Brave" inscribed on it. She had no idea what I was going through, but a simple little necklace and card brought LIFE to me. Her encouraging words, that probably took her all of five minutes to write, brought me so much strength to keep fighting and keep trusting.

As women, it's no secret we all lead busy lives; and when you read things like, "Take the time to do it," you cringe; because in your mind you think, "I have no more time to give." Sisters, it's not a matter of more time; it's a matter of spending our time on things that matter. Let's be women who are obedient to the Holy Spirit's leading.

So many times, the Lord has dropped a way to encourage another woman in my spirit while I am sweeping my kitchen floor. God is always speaking, but we have to have ears to hear Him. We never know what battle other people are fighting, so it's important to always have an encouraging spirit. Maybe that's telling the cashier she's doing a great job even when you've waited in line with screaming kids for twenty minutes. Maybe that's calling someone on the phone and just taking the time to listen. There are so many simple ways we can show encouragement.

To be an encouraging woman, we simply need to remain aware of what's going on around us, and be obedient when the Lord tells us to do or say something. We may not be able to see everyone's battles, but He knows their struggles intimately and knows exactly what they need. The beauty is He chooses to use us to bring life-giving encouragement to others. He wants us to be His hands and feet. Don't you want to be used by God in someone else's life? Yeah, me too!

Prayer

Father, thank You for wanting to use me. Thank You that You care for each one of Your children as individuals. You see what we need and how we need it. Will You use me today, Lord, to bring life to someone? Help me to be alert and ready to be used by You at any moment. In Jesus' name, amen.

SAY IT: *I am Encouraging.*

READ IT: 1 Thessalonians 5:11

WRITE IT: List some ways you can be an encouragement to others. I personally like to send out audio prayers via text to people. Hearing someone call your name out in prayer to God can bring so much joy and peace in the midst of chaos. Whatever way God is leading you to encourage someone today, just be obedient.

day 34

She is Forgiven

"If we claim to be without sin, we deceive ourselves and the truth is not in us. If we confess our sins, he is faithful and just and will forgive us from our sins and purify us from all unrighteousness."

1 JOHN 1:8-9

*I*f we want to be women who are confident in who we are, we must first be women who receive Jesus' forgiveness. Many times the devil likes to play a movie in our heads of all the bad things we have ever done. You would think we would be able to recognize the movie as soon as the previews start, but instead, we grab the popcorn and settle in to watch...over and over again. Then we start telling ourselves we will never amount to anything because of all the things we have done in our past. These are lies, ladies—with a capital L. Recognize them for what they are.

When we feel unforgiven, we tend to draw away from God and His good plan for our lives. I know this all too well,

She is...

because it happened to me for so many years. I allowed the devil to keep me in bondage because of my past. When I was 18 years old, I partied a lot and made a lot of mistakes that many people don't know about. I knew Jesus forgave me for those things, but I just couldn't get past it. I allowed the devil to convince me that my past controlled my future.

The truth is, Jesus Christ died a brutal death on the cross so that you and I can walk in forgiveness. Walking in forgiveness means shame and guilt are not an option. 1 John tells us that we will make mistakes—we are all sinners—but God, in His rich mercy and grace, is just to forgive us every single time we ask.

Make no mistake, the devil does whatever he can to make us feel unqualified to be used by God. He loves it when we talk down to ourselves and relive our past, because then we won't move forward. We'll stay where we're at. The devil wants us to not feel worthy enough to tell people about Jesus. Sister, can I just grab hold of your face for a minute and say, "You are worthy."

Next time you start to feel unforgivable, I want you to look at yourself in the mirror and say, "You are forgiven." Make a choice today to not remain in bondage to your past mistakes and failures. When we realize the power of God's forgiveness in our own lives, it becomes a little easier to forgive others. Choose grace today and move forward, friends. Don't look back!

144

Prayer

Father, if there is anything I need to ask forgiveness for today, please reveal it to me. God, help me to receive Your forgiveness as a precious gift and be confident in that. Let me be a woman who is quick to offer forgiveness because You are always so quick to offer it to me. In Jesus' name, amen.

SAY IT: *I am Forgiven.*

READ IT: 1 John 1:8

WRITE IT: Is there anyone you have not forgiven? A family member, friend, or maybe even yourself? Take some time today to write down the names of the people you need to forgive. Your own name may be on that list. Then, extend the gift of forgiveness; but most importantly, take time today to receive forgiveness.

day 35

She is Generous

*"She opens her arms to the poor and
extends her hands to the needy."*

PROVERBS 31:20

I was sitting at home one day, minding my own business, when I felt the Holy Spirit speaking to me. It was so loud that no one could convince me it was anything else. He was nudging me to give some of my clothes away. "What? Not again! I just cleaned out my closet and took a whole load to the local thrift store." Don't you just love how we plead with God like He will change His mind?

I decided to obey. I opened my closet and looked for the "too tight" clothes. I knew they had to be here somewhere, especially since I had recently been eating too many Little Debbie cakes. There I was digging through all these clothes, and the Holy Spirit again said, "Ivy, give your clothes away." To which I promptly replied, "Ummm, *hellooo!* Lord, that is

147

exactly what I am doing here!"

Then He spoke again: "No, not the clothes you don't like or the ones that are out of style or the ones that no longer fit. Give the ones you love away." With my jaw on the floor, and my heart sinking, I picked out some nice, fitting, trendy, loved (by me) clothes to give away.

That day, I delivered a whole bag of pretty clothes to a single mom who was struggling to survive and care for her children. She was working two jobs and could barely make ends meet. The gratitude she expressed overwhelmed me. It has forever changed me. I was so honored God would use me to bring so much happiness to this mama.

Sometimes I think God asks us to do things outside our comfort zone to show us how much simple obedience cannot only change the person we are blessing, but also how much it can change us. Get this: I later had a pastor come up to me and give me $100 to go buy myself some new clothes. That pastor knew nothing about the time I gave those clothes to that mama in need, but God knew; and He honored my obedience.

Giving clothes away is not the only way to be generous. We can be generous with our time, our money, our ears, our homes, and our love. The way to become a generous woman is to just always be obedient to whatever it is that God is calling you to do, even if it means giving away your favorite shirt. Sigh.

Prayer

God, thank You for all that You have given me. You have blessed me so much, and I want to always be a generous woman. You are so good to me and love me so much. Help me today to be generous with everything You've given me. In Jesus' name, amen.

SAY IT: *I am Generous.*

READ IT: Proverbs 31:20, Proverbs 11:24-25

WRITE IT: What are some ways you can be generous today? Get your pen and paper ready, and ask the Lord to speak to you.

day 36

She is Trustworthy

*"Her husband has full confidence in her
and lacks nothing of value."*

PROVERBS 31:11

There is nothing that brings me greater joy than when my husband is proud of me. I love when I can show up and show out on a job he has entrusted me to do. I love knowing he can trust me. Knowing he has confidence in me gives me confidence in myself. Friends, the road to becoming a trustworthy woman requires confidence, openness, and honesty. Being trustworthy isn't just about being really good at keeping secrets. It's also about knowing who you are so that people have confidence in you.

The definition of *trustworthy* is "to be able to be relied on as honest or truthful." Does this describe you? Another definition of *trustworthy* is "deserving of trust or able to be trusted." Think

151

about those two meanings, and ask yourself, "What has God trusted me to do?"

Maybe God has trusted you to raise world changers. Has God trusted you to be a Godly wife and cover your husband in prayer daily? Has He trusted you to write a book? Has He trusted you with the ability to teach? Whatever it is that God has trusted you to do, are you doing it? Are you using the gifts and talents He's given you and following Him obediently in every area of your life? Are you proving yourself to be trustworthy?

Ladies, we must ask ourselves these hard questions in order to grow. If we don't want to become stale and stagnant women (Where's the fun in that?!), we must always be asking ourselves, "Am I living out God's call on my life?" Let's do it! Let's ask God to reveal His calling on our lives. Let's be obedient in following Him, and let's make a choice today to be known as trustworthy women.

Prayer

Father, forgive me for the moments I have not proven myself to be trustworthy. I pray You would help me grow in this area. Help me to steward well the talents and tasks You give me. I need your Holy Sprit to remind me of what is true. I love you, Jesus. Thank You for being so good to me. In Jesus' name, amen.

SAY IT: *I am Trustworthy.*

READ IT: Proverbs 31:11, Proverbs 10:9

WRITE IT: We can't change what we don't acknowledge. Make a list today of all the things God has trusted you with—your husband, your children, your home, your career, etc. Hang this list in a place where you will see it every day as a reminder that you have an important part to play. Play it well!

day 37

She is Selfless

"You, my brothers and sisters, were called to be free.
But do not use your freedom to indulge the flesh.
Rather, serve one another humbly in love."

GALATIANS 5:13

As moms, we tend to have selfless spirits. We will run ourselves ragged for the sake of our children. We'll deny our hair, fashion sense, hot meals, sleep, alone time in the bathroom, and the list goes on and on… But that same selfless spirit often goes right out the window when it comes to our husbands, friends, or co-workers. Why do we pout when things don't go our way? Where does this attitude of entitlement come from?

My pastor recently preached an amazing sermon series titled "It's Not About Me." It was such a good reminder that life is not about me; and it's not all about you either. Life is about reaching the lost, growing in our walk with the Lord, loving people, and making disciples. In order to do these things, there are many moments when we will have to die to ourselves.

It's a pretty universal desire to want to be recognized for the good things we do, but why do we really need people to applaud and shout our name? We often want the credit because we are simply making life all about us. Jesus said He came to this earth to serve, not to be served. If Jesus, the Son of God, said that, don't you think there is truth in that for us, too?

Let us be women who pray for God to show us ways to be selfless. I know, I know... The thought gives you a headache. It's so much easier to just look out for me, myself, and I; because that's where it's most comfortable. But sister, we are not called to comfort.

In order for God to increase in our lives, we have to decrease. You cannot fill a full jar. If it's full, then the stuff you are trying to fill it with will not stay inside. In the same way, we must ask God to pull the selfishness out of us and replace it with His kind of selflessness. Here's the truth: God will always show us ways to dig that root of selfishness out. We just have to listen and obey when He starts talking. Are you ready? Let's do it together.

Prayer

*Father, show me the areas in my life where I am selfish. I pray,
God, You will show me the big ways, and even the small ways,
where I am selfish. In order to uproot something, I know You
have to dig deep and start at the source. God, I am digging deep
today. Begin a work in me. I want to decrease so that You may
increase. In Your name I pray, amen.*

SAY IT: *I am Selfless.*

READ IT: Galatians 5:13

WRITE IT: Today's challenge involves more doing than
writing. Make an effort today to be as selfless as you can.
Start putting selflessness into practice. Let your friend pick
the restaurant—and don't complain about her choice. Do
something nice for your husband—without expectations of
anything in return. Let someone go ahead of you in the grocery
check-out line. These acts may all seem trivial, but if we can't be
selfless in the little things, then we sure won't be selfless in the
big things. Remember, we are uprooting this thing!

day 38

She is Gracious

"A kindhearted woman gains honor,
but ruthless men gain only wealth."

PROVERBS 11:16

It is only by God's grace that we are saved. He looked down on us, in all our brokenness and sin, and still chose us. It is because of His grace that He sent Jesus to earth to be beaten and ridiculed so that we could live with Him forever. This is the Gospel, ladies! This is something we should never lose our excitement over. When we no longer get excited about this precious gift, then we need to just sit down. The Gospel of this gracious love should compel us to tell as many people as we possibly can about Jesus!

God gives us a perfect example of gracious living. How often do we look at the sins of other people and think they don't deserve our kindness, forgiveness, or grace? Spoiler alert! We don't deserve the grace God shows us on a daily basis. How can we possibly not extend it to others?

This became a huge reality to me once I had children. There are times when my five year old disobeys me, lies, hits his little brother, tears something up that I told him not to touch…the list goes on and on. But do all these things change the way I feel about him? Absolutely not! There is nothing that boy can do to waver my love for him.

I want to become very vulnerable with you here. Remember earlier in the book when I told you I partied a lot when I was 18? Well, in that time I also had sex with a few guys. I gave myself away in moments of being drunk, trying to cope with my brokenness and what was going on at home. Noah knew nothing of this. I couldn't bear to let him see this side of me—this broken and nasty part of me—because he was a Godly man. (These were all lies from the enemy to keep me in bondage, by the way.)

It wasn't until five years into our marriage that I told him this dirty secret of mine. I let the devil lie to me for so many years, telling me, "You weren't married then, so he doesn't have to know." "He will leave you." "He will not look at you the same." Lie after lie silenced me year after year. Finally, I had had enough! I told him. I braced for the worst, but I also felt complete freedom. In a moment I thought, *Surely my husband will forsake me,* he did just the opposite. He loved me and told me he was so thankful I told him, because he never wanted me to go through all those years alone. It was the very essence of God's love being shown through my precious husband. He was so gracious to me. I believe he was able to do this because he has seen God be so gracious to him so many times. Our marriage has never been stronger!

When we get to the place where we realize we are all broken, helpless, wrecked people in need of a Savior, then we will start to see people through the eyes of God. We will start to treat them with grace. We will begin to treat everyone with love and compassion—the same love and compassion that is freely given to us every single day by our Father in heaven.

Prayer

Father, help me to see Your face when I look at people. Jesus, help me to be very quick to show grace. Help me to be kind to all people, no matter what. I want to be a part of bringing a gracious spirit to everyone I meet, and I know that I can't do that without You, Jesus. In the name of Your Son I pray, amen.

SAY IT: *I am Gracious.*

READ IT: Proverbs 11:16, Ephesians 2:8-9

WRITE IT: Have there been times when you haven't shown grace to others? Sometimes it helps to remember the places God has brought us from so that when it's our turn to show grace, we will extend it quickly and generously. Describe a few moments in your life where Jesus showered you with love and grace, even though you deserved far worse. Our salvation should be at the top of that list!

day 39

She is Faithful

"Whoever can be trusted with very little can also be trusted with very much, and whoever is dishonest with very little will be dishonest with very much."

LUKE 16:10

We have all heard the saying, "God is faithful!" He most certainly is! But have you ever considered that as women of God, He expects you and me to be faithful, too?

One day while cleaning my house for what felt like the thousandth time, I walked into my son's room only to find a bright red stain on the floor. I have no idea why red coloring in food or drinks is even a thing. Nothing good ever comes from it.

I was so mad! Here I was cleaning this house like a maid servant, and what do I get in return? More mess! That's when I heard the Holy Spirit whisper to me, "Just be faithful."

"Ummm, excuse me, Lord. I *am* being faithful. Do you not

see me on my hands and knees faithfully scrubbing this devil color out of the carpet?"

In that moment, I was reminded that the Bible tells us that whatever we do, we should do it for the Lord. Being faithful sometimes means you just keep pressing on even when things get hard. Everything in life is seasonal, and it's really important that we remember that. Crumbs and spills and "Oops, Mommy!" moments won't last forever. Don't let the devil rattle you about something that one day you'll look back on and laugh about.

Let's be faithful in our prayer life, too. (Carpet stains will increase your prayer life!) Let's be women who faithfully spend time with Jesus, serving Him (and others), and constantly giving thanks for His goodness in our lives. Yes, scrubbing floors may step on our last nerve that's only hanging on by a thread anyway, but at least we have floors! Always make a choice to find the good.

God wants us to enjoy our life, not just merely exist; and I am finding that the more I embrace whatever season He has me in and serve Him faithfully for as long as that season lasts, I have joy—even when life is hard. So today, choose to be faithful. Wake up each morning with thanksgiving in your heart, and spend time with your Creator. He loves you so very much, and He continues to be so faithful.

Prayer

Thank You, Jesus, for Your faithfulness. You are faithful even when I am not. Help me today to do all that I do faithfully as if I am serving You. Jesus, help me to embrace each and every season that I go through so that I can find Your joy there. Thank You for loving me. In Jesus' name, amen.

SAY IT: *I am Faithful.*

READ IT: Luke 16:10

WRITE IT: What are some things in your life that you are faithfully doing every day, but you need God to renew your strength to keep doing them? Make a list, and then pray over it. Ask God to renew your spirit and to help you move forward doing these tasks with excitement and joy because you are doing them for Him and not for anyone else.

day 40

She is Noble

"A wife of noble character who can find?"
PROVERBS 31:10

When I hear the word noble, I think of a royal princess, one with infinite class and etiquette. One who walks as if she is walking on clouds, so delicate and dainty. Her hair blows in the wind, and her dresses are always a perfect fit. This girl's a princess who is respected in all her land and lives in her fairytale castle with her Prince Charming.

OK, let me just stop my delusion right here, because if this is the type of woman Proverbs is looking for, then I just ain't fittin' the bill! I'm not dainty and delicate. I rarely get through a meal without spilling something. I'm as clumsy as they come. My hair has dry shampoo in it on any given day to soak up the grease from not washing it. And my "castle" is a chaotic home where laundry overfloweth.

After doing some research, I found that the word *noble* in

Proverbs actually refers to a woman's character, her morals. Shew! Praise the Lord! My morals and character are things I can totally work on. The other stuff? Well, let's just say I'm settled in my ways.

As Godly women, we are called to look different than other women. Do you appear different than the world? If people looked at your life, compared to an unsaved person's life, would they see any difference? These are tough questions to ask, but in order to grow in the Lord, we have to be honest with ourselves and see if there is anything about our lives that sets us apart. Our lives *should* look different.

Are the morals you base your life on lined up with biblical truth, or are they just your opinions? To be women of noble character, we must know the truth; and the truth must be in us. If we live by the truth of God's Word, we will look different than the rest of the world. People should know you are a Christian, not because you say, "I love God," but because you show you love God with your life.

A noble woman knows her Creator and follows His commands. Proverbs asks, "Who can find such a woman?" Ever wonder why it says, "Who can find?" I would venture to say it's because there are a lot of women who claim to be women of upstanding character and morals, but when it comes right down to it, they are just lying to themselves.

Choose today whom you will serve. Will it be God and His Word, or will you just stay comfortable and live like the rest of the world?

Friends, we are called to be different. We are commanded to practice Godly morals and live our lives as testimonies for others. Let's be that woman today—the modern-day princess who is a beautiful mess but known by her love for Jesus.

Prayer

God, help me become a woman of noble character. Convict my heart on anything that could be un-Godly and might be causing others to stumble. Let my character and lifestyle show Jesus to all who watch me. In Jesus' name, amen.

SAY IT: *I am Noble.*

READ IT: Proverbs 31 (Just read the whole chapter—it's so worth it!)

WRITE IT: What are some morals you are unsure about? Maybe you have questions about certain lifestyles that are considered acceptable to the world but not acceptable to God. Write your questions down, and do your homework! Dig into the Word, google, and ask a wiser friend to help you. But, most importantly, ask God to reveal His truth to you.

day 41

She is Qualified

"Being strengthened with all power according to his glorious might so that you may have great endurance and patience. And giving joyful thanks to the father, who has qualified you to share in the inheritance of his holy people in the kingdom of light."

COLOSSIANS 1:11-12

When Jesus set out to choose His disciples, He didn't go looking for the people who came from wealthy families, religious leaders or teachers, or the people with the most talent. The disciples Jesus chose were fishermen. To understand how powerful this is, you have to understand the culture back in that day. It was every Jewish boy's dream, and duty for that matter, to learn the Torah so he could follow and learn from a rabbi. If you were not capable of learning Jewish law, then you might fall back into your family trade; and that's what you would be "stuck" doing for the rest of your life.

So, as Jesus went through and handpicked each one of his

twelve disciples, He would have known these were the guys who "failed," so to speak, in their culture. They weren't studying theology. They were average guys, working hard in the family business. But guess what? Jesus said, "Yep! I'll take him!" Wow, that's powerful! Although they were not qualified by human standards, Jesus said they were qualified through Him.

Jesus does the same thing for you and me. There have been so many times in my life when I've felt unqualified to do anything for the King of Kings. God will put huge things in my heart for me to do—like, oh you know, write a book—and immediately I begin to tell Him why I cannot do this. But Jesus is always saying to me (and to you), "No, you can't do it; but through Me, you can do anything."

I now understand why the disciples dropped everything to follow Jesus. They left their income, stability, families, and comfort behind immediately, without hesitation. They did this because they saw a rabbi who believed in them, and they knew they needed to trust Him.

It is so important that you know and understand that Jesus Christ believes in you. He believes in His daughters because He knows what He can do through us. He wants us to take the unqualified parts of ourselves and lay them down at His feet. I have known this to be true in my own life. There have been times when I feel there is just no way I can do something, but once I release it to Jesus, He gives me the strength, wisdom, and endurance I need to do it. If He can do it for His twelve disciples, don't you think He can qualify you, too? Yes, honey, He can!

Prayer

Sweet Father in heaven, I pray You would help me to see that You have qualified me. Even on days I do not feel it, Your Word tells me I am qualified. You chose Your twelve disciples, and You also chose me. You love me and want to use me. Thank You for believing in me. Thank You, Jesus, for loving me with an everlasting love. In Jesus' name, amen.

SAY IT: *I am Qualified.*

READ IT: Colossians 1:11-12

WRITE IT: Write these words down on a sticky note: *Jesus qualified me.* Place this note in a highly-trafficked spot in your home so that you will always remember who believes in you and qualifies you.

day 42

She is Disciplined

"No discipline seems pleasant at the time, but painful.
Later on however it produces a harvest of righteousness and peace
for those who have been trained by it."
Hebrews 12:11

As parents, there are times when my husband and I have to redirect our children. It is our responsibility to show them when they are doing something wrong. With the leading of the Holy Spirit, we are their teachers and their guides as they walk through life. Our ultimate goal is that our children learn from our direction and use it to better their adult lives.

God does the same thing with His children. God is our Father, and He tells us in His Word that He disciplines the ones He loves. So why is it that when God starts trying to teach us something we immediately say, "That devil is at me again!"? Have you ever considered that maybe it's not the devil at all? Maybe when we're thrown a curveball, God is trying to take us through something that will bring a harvest of righteousness in our lives.

I recently joined a gym. Apparently as you age, your body starts holding onto weight that used to come off quickly. Suddenly, I can no longer eat Oreos, go for a light walk, and still lose weight. Nevertheless, I joined and decided I would have to start letting my body know who was in charge here.

The first week I was super nervous, so I did the only natural thing to do. I found the most fit looking female in that gym and did what she did. I wouldn't recommend that, because apparently she had been working out for years; and here I was a newbie trying to keep up. My body ached all over the next morning. I could not even sit on the potty; I just fell onto it. When I first started working out, I was in pain; but now, a few months into it, regular exercise brings strength and endurance. I'm starting to see the fruit of additional energy and actual weight loss.

It's never pleasant when God allows us to exercise our faith through difficult seasons; but these seasons are necessary to grow in Jesus. If I want to experience the benefits of the gym, I have to put in the work. I have to train my body to endure the beating I give it. But in the end, my body thanks me. The same rules apply to our faith. If we want to see the benefits of our faith, we have to exercise it.

Remember when the disciples went through a horrible storm in Mark 4? Jesus led them there, but here's the key: He was in the boat, and He was the one who calmed the storm. No matter what you're going through today, Jesus is in your boat, sister! The more you exercise your faith in the midst of your storm, the closer you will get to Christ. Let's be women who stay teachable, allowing our Father to discipline us so that we become all He's created us to be!

Prayer

Jesus, thank You for teaching me discipline. Thank You for giving me a spirit of self-discipline. You have already put inside of me all that I need to endure anything. Help me to remember You discipline the ones You love, so no matter what I walk through, You can teach me something in every season and circumstance. In Jesus' name, amen.

SAY IT: *I am Disciplined.*

READ IT: Hebrews 12:11, 2 Timothy 1:7

WRITE IT: Make a list of some areas in your life where you need to put self-discipline into play. Next, make a list of some areas in your life where you feel God is trying to teach you something. What lessons are you learning through His loving discipline?

We made it! I pray the last forty-two days have challenged and strengthened you. I pray that you can look at yourself in the mirror and see God's masterpiece. Remember, when God looks down at you from heaven, He holds your face in His hands and says, "I love you with an everlasting love. I cherish you. I value you. You are mine." May we cling tightly to the truth of who He says we are!

I do hate goodbyes, so let's not end this book that way. I mean, we have spent a whole forty-two days together, so we are basically best friends at this point! You don't tell your best friend goodbye; instead you say, "See you later!" So sister, that is what I say to you.

See you later! xoxo,

Ivy

About the Author

IVY CLEVELAND is founder of She Is Ministries and the author of *She Is* and *Warrior Girl*. As a speaker, she has spoken at women's events all over the United States. She has a passion to help women see their full potential and who God has created them to be. Through humor, vulnerability, and passion her message connects with women of all ages and backgrounds.

She is also the wife of 11 years to national recording artist, Noah Cleveland. They live in Atlanta, GA with their two boys, and are in the process of bringing a third child to a forever home from China. Together they have been to 31 states, ministered to over 250,000 people, and seen over 10,000 people say YES to Jesus. Their heart is to point people Christ.

AVAILABLE NOW

SISTER, DID YOU KNOW THAT WE'RE IN THE MIDDLE OF A WAR?